D0980414

Paris
day BY day

4th Edition

by Anna E. Brooke

FrommerMedia LLC

Contents

Published by:

Frommer Media LLC

Copyright © 2014 Frommer Media LLC, New York, NY. All rights reserved. No part of this publication may be reproduced, stored in a retrieval system or transmitted in any form or by any means, electronic, mechanical, photocopying, recording, scanning or otherwise, except as permitted under Sections 107 or 108 of the 1976 United States Copyright Act, without the prior written permission of the Publisher. Requests to the Publisher for permission should be addressed to http://www.frommers.com/support.

Frommer's is a trademark or registered trademark of Arthur Frommer.

ISBN: 978-1-628-87022-0 (paper); 978-1-628-87052-7 (ebk)

Editorial Director: Pauline Frommer
Editor: Kate Hambrecht
Production Editor: Heather Wilcox
Photo Editor: Seth Olenick
Cartographer: Elizabeth Puhl
Page Compositor: Lissa Auciello-Brogan
Indexer: Kelly Henthorne

For information on our other products and services, please go to Frommers.com/contactus.

Frommer's also publishes its books in a variety of electronic formats. Some content that appears in print may not be available in electronic formats.

Manufactured in China

5   4   3   2

A Note from the Publisher

Organizing your time. That's what this guide is all about.

Other guides give you long lists of things to see and do and then expect you to fit the pieces together. The Day by Day guides are different. These guides tell you the best of everything, and then they show you how to see it *in the smartest, most time-efficient way*. Our authors have designed detailed itineraries organized by time, neighborhood, or special interest. And each tour comes with a bulleted map that takes you from stop to stop.

Hoping to follow Hemingway's footsteps, or to tour the highlights of the Louvre? Planning a walk through Montmartre, or a whirlwind tour of the very best that Paris has to offer? Whatever your interest or schedule, the Day by Days give you the smartest routes to follow. Not only do we take you to the top attractions, hotels, and restaurants, but we also help you access those special moments that locals get to experience—those "finds" that turn tourists into travelers.

The Day by Days are also your top choice if you're looking for one complete guide for all your travel needs. The best hotels and restaurants for every budget, the greatest shopping values, the wildest nightlife—it's all here.

Why should you trust our judgment? Because our authors personally visit each place they write about. They're an independent lot who say what they think and would never include places they wouldn't recommend to their best friends. They're also open to suggestions from readers. If you'd like to contact them, please send your comments our way at Support@FrommerMedia.com, and we'll pass them on.

Enjoy your Day by Day guide—the most helpful travel companion you can buy. And have the trip of a lifetime.

About the Author

British-born **Anna Brooke** moved to Paris in 2000 and hasn't looked back since. She is now a full-fledged bohemian, juggling life between freelance travel writing (Frommer's, *The Sunday Times Travel Magazine, Time Out Paris,* and the *Financial Times*), children's fiction, acting, and songwriting for films for her electro-pop band, Monkey Anna (www.soundcloud.com/monkeyanna).

Advisory & Disclaimer

Travel information can change quickly and unexpectedly, and we strongly advise you to confirm important details locally before traveling, including information on visas, health and safety, traffic and transport, accommodations, shopping, and eating out. We also encourage you to stay alert while traveling and to remain aware of your surroundings. Avoid civil disturbances, and keep a close eye on cameras, purses, wallets, and other valuables.

While we have endeavored to ensure that the information contained within this guide is accurate and up-to-date at the time of publication, we make no representations or warranties with respect to the accuracy or completeness of the contents of this work and specifically disclaim all warranties, including without limitation warranties of fitness for a particular purpose. We accept no responsibility or liability for any inaccuracy or errors or omissions, or for any inconvenience, loss, damage, costs, or expenses of any nature whatsoever incurred or suffered by anyone as a result of any advice or information contained in this guide.

The inclusion of a company, organization, or website in this guide as a service provider and/or potential source of further information does not mean that we endorse them or the information they provide. Be aware that information provided through some websites may be unreliable and can change without notice. Neither the publisher nor author shall be liable for any damages arising herefrom.

Star Ratings, Icons & Abbreviations

Every hotel, restaurant, and attraction listing in this guide has been ranked for quality, value, service, amenities, and special features using a **star-rating system.** Hotels, restaurants, attractions, shopping, and nightlife are rated on a scale of zero stars (recommended) to three stars (exceptional). In addition to the star-rating system, we also use a **kids** icon to point out the best bets for families. Within each tour, we recommend cafes, bars, or restaurants where you can take a break. Each of these stops appears in a shaded box marked with a coffee-cup-shaped bullet 🍵.

The following **abbreviations** are used for credit cards:

AE	American Express	DISC	Discover	V	Visa
DC	Diners Club	MC	MasterCard		

Frommers.com

Now that you have this guidebook to help you plan a great trip, visit our website at **www.frommers.com** for additional travel information on more than 4,000 destinations. We update features regularly to give you instant access to the most current trip-planning information available. At Frommers.com, you'll find scoops on the best airfares, lodging rates, and car rental bargains. You can even book your travel online through our reliable travel booking partners. Other popular features include:

- Online updates of our most popular guidebooks
- Vacation sweepstakes and contest giveaways
- Newsletters highlighting the hottest travel trends
- Podcasts, interactive maps, and up-to-the-minute event listings
- Opinionated blog entries by Arthur Frommer himself
- Online travel message boards with featured travel discussions

A Note on Prices

In the "Take a Break" (coffee-cup icon) and "Best Bets" sections of this book, we have used a system of dollar signs to show a range of costs for 1 night in a hotel (the price of a double-occupancy room) or the cost of an entree at a restaurant. Use the following table to decipher the dollar signs:

Cost	Hotels	Restaurants
$	under $100	under $10
$$	$100–$200	$10–$20
$$$	$200–$300	$20–$30
$$$$	$300–$400	$30–$40
$$$$$	over $400	over $40

How to Contact Us

In researching this book, we discovered many wonderful places—hotels, restaurants, shops, and more. We're sure you'll find others. Please tell us about them, so we can share the information with your fellow travelers in upcoming editions. If you were disappointed with a recommendation, we'd love to know that, too. Please write to: Support@FrommerMedia.com

13 Favorite
Moments

2

Favorite Moments

Favorite Moments

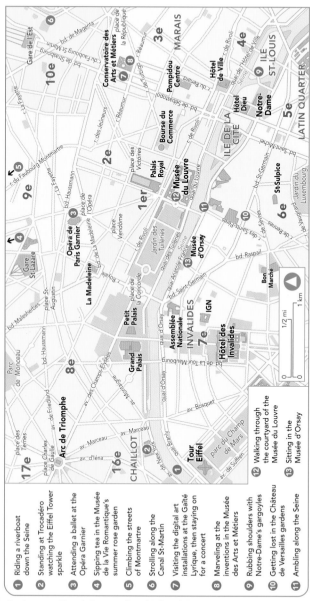

1 Riding a riverboat down the Seine

2 Standing at Trocadéro watching the Eiffel Tower sparkle

3 Attending a ballet at the Opéra Garnier

4 Sipping tea in the Musée de la Vie Romantique's summer rose garden

5 Climbing the streets of Montmartre

6 Strolling along the Canal St-Martin

7 Visiting the digital art installations at the Gaîté Lyrique, then staying on for a concert

8 Marveling at the inventions in the Musée des Arts et Métiers

9 Rubbing shoulders with Notre-Dame's gargoyles

10 Getting lost in the Château de Versailles gardens

11 Ambling along the Seine

12 Walking through the courtyard of the Musée du Louvre

13 Sitting in the Musée d'Orsay

Previous page: Tour de France cyclists whiz through Paris.

Waiting for the Eiffel Tower to light up after dark, strolling along the Seine on a warm summer night—these could become your favorite moments in the world, not just in Paris. This is an electric city—a "moveable feast" (as Ernest Hemingway so aptly called it). The list of wonderful experiences to be had here is endless. Here are 13 of my favorites.

① Walking through the courtyard of the Musée du Louvre early in the morning, hurrying to be one of the first in line, and catching the sun glinting off the glass pyramids in the courtyard—it only heightens the excitement of seeing the masterpieces inside. *See p 30.*

② Visiting the digital art installations at the Gaîté Lyrique, then staying on for a concert. It's a great way to check out Paris's red-hot electronic music scene and meet locals interested in the newest art on the block—digital art, which covers everything from computer graphics and animation to experimental video. *See p 133.*

③ Ambling along the Seine toward the islands, watching the tour boats *(bateaux mouches)* cruise slowly by, the lights from their windows reflecting on the river. On summer nights, the riverside is packed, even after 10pm; sometimes it seems as if everybody in Paris is here. Bands play, lovers kiss, children frolic, everybody smiles—this is how life should be all the time. *See p 135.*

④ Sitting in the Musée d'Orsay in the center sculpture court, down below the entrance, looking up at the huge, ornate clock on the wall far above. Through the frosted glass around it, you can see the shadows of people passing by on invisible walkways. The sheer scale is astounding; the look is pure drama. And all around you, the works of history's most talented sculptors lounge, leap, and laugh silently. *See p 7.*

⑤ Strolling along the Canal St-Martin, passing delicate iron bridges, locks, and the occasional fisherman. You could spend the better part of a day losing yourself in the bohemian boutiques, stopping at a cafe, and then continuing along to the Parc de la Villette for a picnic in the park or a trip around the *Cité des Sciences. See p 68.*

⑥ Sipping tea in the Musée de la Vie Romantique's summer rose garden. The pink, ivy-clad house once frequented by George Sand and Frédéric Chopin feels like Paris's best-kept secret. Visit the museum and then wind down in the

A leisurely stroll along the Seine.

garden over a Darjeeling tea and a *tarte du jour*, with just the buzzing of bees and the clinking of tea cups for company. *See p 38.*

⑦ **Getting lost in the Château de Versailles gardens.** This opulent château of the Sun King, Louis XIV, was the *bijou* (jewel) in the royal crown. Nowadays it is the glittering highlight of any visit to the Île-de-France. Nothing can beat a day spent ambling through the terraced gardens, admiring the fountains and Marie Antoinette's hamlet. Classical music extravaganzas take place there during the warmer months. *See p 155,* ②.

⑧ **Climbing the streets of Montmartre.** This hilly, hopelessly romantic neighborhood is my favorite in all of Paris. A sweeping view of the city spreads out before you from every cross street. Every corner reveals another evocative stone staircase too steep to see all the way down, but at the bottom you know you'll find sweet old buildings painted pale colors and streets of old paving stones. *See p 64.*

⑨ **Standing at Trocadéro watching the Eiffel Tower sparkle** at nightfall. It's the best place in town to take in the tower's elegant, filigree proportions, and that moment

Don your finest attire for a night out at Opéra Garnier.

when somebody, somewhere, flicks the button is matchless. *See p 24.*

⑩ **Attending a ballet at the Opéra Garnier.** Whether you're seeing a traditional rendition of Tchaikovsky's *The Nutcracker* or a contemporary version of Prokofiev's *Romeo et Juliette,* the Charles Garnier–designed grande dame of performance spaces provides a breathtaking backdrop for ballet. Climb the majestic central staircase, order champagne for the *entr'acte* (intermission), and then sink into your red velvet chair and admire Chagall's famous ceiling fresco before the lights go down. *See p 135.*

⑪ **Rubbing shoulders with Notre-Dame's gargoyles.** Climb the uneven stone steps to the top of Notre-Dame's towers, and you're in the precipitous realm of Quasimodo, where hideous stone sculptures stick out their tongues at the city below. The views from here are mesmerizing, especially on a cloudy day, when the sky looks moody. *See p 9,* ⑦.

⑫ **Riding a riverboat down the Seine,** where all the buildings are artfully lighted so they seem to glow from within. On warm nights, take an open-top boat and feel as if you can reach up and touch the damp, stone bridges as you pass beneath them. *See p 11.*

⑬ **Marveling at the inventions in the Musée des Arts et Métiers.** This museum is easy to miss, yet it contains some of the world's greatest inventions: Blaise Pascal's 17th-century calculator, the *Blériot 11* (the first plane to cross the English Channel), steam-powered carriages, and Henry Ford's Model T car and automated looms. It's a must-see for science fans big and small. *See p 39,* ⑥. ●

1 The Best Full-Day Tours

The Best **in One Day**

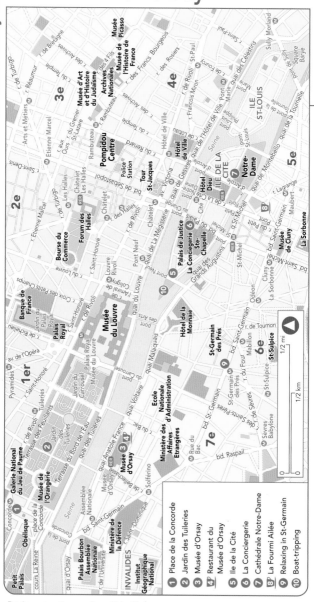

1 Place de la Concorde
2 Jardin des Tuileries
3 Musée d'Orsay
4 Restaurant du Musée d'Orsay
5 Ile de la Cité
6 La Conciergerie
7 Cathédrale Notre-Dame
8 La Fourmi Ailée
9 Relaxing in St-Germain
10 Boat-tripping

Previous page: A gargoyle on Notre-Dame.

From the fountain-strewn expanses of Place de la Concorde, a mosaic of elegant squares, palaces, and parks unfurls. Once you've spent some time with the Musée d'Orsay's 19th-century masterpieces, the narrow cobblestone streets of Paris's islands beckon before pointing you toward a cafe terrace in Saint-Germain for pre-dinner drinks. For this whirlwind 1-day tour, I aim to show you everything I would want to see if I had only 24 hours in the City of Light. It's an ambitious itinerary, so start early and wear comfortable shoes. START: **Métro to Concorde.**

1 ★★ Place de la Concorde. From the city's largest square, you get immediate Paris gratification. First, admire the view of the Eiffel Tower, and then position yourself to see down the Champs Elysées to the Arc de Triomphe, a monument to Napoleon's conquests. Behind you are the Tuileries gardens and the Louvre museum. To your left, you'll see the Madeleine Church—a mirror image of the Assemblée Nationale across the Seine (home to the lower house of the French Parliament). Amid the fountains, tourists, and traffic stands the 3,300-year-old Luxor Obelisk (a gift from Egypt in 1829), placed on the spot where once stood the guillotine that executed thousands during the Revolution. This lovely viewpoint is your own instant postcard. Welcome to Paris. ⏱ *10 min. Go early in the morning to avoid crowds or just after sunset to see the edifices aglow. Free admission. Métro: Concorde.*

2 Jardin des Tuileries. Place de la Concorde ends where the Louvre's stately sculpture-strewn gardens begin. On a space about the size of two football fields, chestnut trees shade winding paths. It's a beautiful place to walk, read, or admire sculptures by such greats as Rodin and Maillol. See also the "Jardin des Tuileries" tour on p 90. ⏱ *20 min. Summer daily 7am–9pm, winter daily 7am–nightfall. Métro: Tuileries or Concorde.*

3 ★★★ Musée d'Orsay. Just across the Seine is the Gare d'Orsay, the old Belle Epoque train station built for the 1900 exposition and later turned into a museum devoted to works created from 1848 to 1914. Fans of Impressionism will be in paradise amid masterpieces by Manet, Renoir, Degas, Cézanne, and Monet. The Post-Impressionist collection includes pieces by van Gogh, Seurat, Rousseau, and

An overview of the Musée d'Orsay, in a converted train station.

Gargoyles from the pont Neuf.

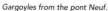

Gauguin. A huge, ornate clock dominates the light-filled central hall. Statues of robust maidens and eager men stand where the train tracks once lay, including Carpeaux's *La Danse* (once controversial for its frolicking nude figures). ⏱ *2–3 hr. 1 rue de la Légion d'Honneur, 7th.* ☎ *01-40-49-48-14. www.musee-orsay.fr. Admission 9€ ages 26 & over, 6.50€ ages 18–25, free for children 17 & under and visitors 25 & under from E.U. countries. Tues–Wed & Fri–Sun 9:30am–6pm, Thurs 9:30am–9:45pm. Métro: Solférino & Assemblée Nationale. RER: Musée d'Orsay.*

4 ★ **Restaurant du Musée d'Orsay.** Breakfast and lunch are served in the Musée d'Orsay's bustling first-floor restaurant—a gorgeous Belle Epoque dining room. Between 2:45 and 5pm, enjoy a slice of chocolate cake and a cup of tea. *$.*

5 ★★★ **Île de la Cité.** One of the most Parisian things you can do is stroll along the Seine to the Île de la Cité, the birthplace of Paris. Take a right as you leave the Musée d'Orsay. It's about a 15-minute walk to this island, home to **Notre-Dame**

Cathedral. Cross onto the island at the **pont Neuf** (New Bridge), which despite its name is the oldest bridge in the city; note the statue of Henri IV, who commissioned the *pont* in 1578. To your right will be the pretty pink Place Dauphine. At the far end of the square is the west wing of the **Palais de Justice,** Paris's law courts (Rue de Harlay). This is an active court building, so unfortunately tourists are not welcome. But you can admire the majestic east facade (the main entrance) behind gilded gates, between the Conciergerie and Sainte-Chapelle on the next stop of this tour. ⏱ *30 min. Métro: Pont Neuf.*

6 ★★ **La Conciergerie.** The fairy-tale towers that soar above the north end of the island near the pont Neuf lead you to the fortress where Marie Antoinette was imprisoned before her execution, now a museum. Its intimidating look is largely courtesy of an 1850s makeover, but most of the building is much older—several parts date to the 12th and 13th centuries, when it was a royal palace. During the French Revolution, torture and execution were commonplace here, and it became a symbol of terror.

Budget Paris in 1 Day

Believe it or not, it is possible to spend a day in Paris with just 20€ in your pocket. Start your morning amid France's second-largest collection of Chinese art at the fabulous and free **Musée Cernuschi**, 7 av. Vélasquez, 8th (☎ 01-53-96-21-50; www.cernuschi.paris.fr; free admission; Tues–Sun 10am–6pm; Métro: Villiers or Monceau). The collection ranges from Neolithic terra cottas and Wei dynasty funeral statues (A.D. 386–534) to Sung porcelain and rare gold Liao dynasty objets d'art (A.D. 907–1125). Then, if the weather is fair, find a place in the sun for an early picnic lunch at the **Parc Monceau** next door. This elegant oasis ringed with stately mansions was designed by writer, artist, and architect Louis Carrogis Carmontelle in 1778 as a hideaway for the duke of Chartres. Admire the Roman columns and a small Egyptian pyramid as you tuck into your baguette. If you haven't bought your food yet, consider the street market on Rue de Lévis by the Villiers Métro stop (access on bd. de Courcelles, av. Vélasquez, av. Van Dyck & av. Ruysdaël; Métro: Monceau or Villiers). If it's cold or rainy, opt for Les Caves Populaires, at 22 rue des Dames, 17th (☎ 01-53-04-08-32; Mon–Sat 8am–2am, Sun 11am–2am; Métro: Place de Clichy). This rustic local haunt on one of Paris's most bohemian streets is the perfect spot for a coffee or a glass of wine—a steal starting at just 2.50€. After your meal, while away the afternoon amid the arty streets of **Montmartre.** At the highest point in Paris, this village within the city affords incomparable views. For dinner, you'll find some of the best no-frills French cuisine in town at **Chartier,** 7 rue du Faubourg Montmartre, 9th (p 108). Just be prepared for very long queues.

You can visit cells in which prisoners were held (including a reconstruction of Marie Antoinette's) as well as the former banquet halls and guardrooms. Next door is the medieval **Sainte-Chapelle** (buy a dual ticket upon arrival), one of the most beautiful chapels you'll ever see. It's famous for the breathtaking "light show" cast on the interior when the sun shines through the stained-glass windows. ⏱ *1 hr. 2 bd. du Palais, 1st.* ☎ *01-53-40-60-80. www.conciergerie.monuments-nationaux.fr. Admission 8.50€ (13€ dual ticket) ages 26 & over, 5.50€ ages 18–25 (8.50€ dual ticket), free for children 17 & under. Daily 9am–6pm. Métro: Cité.*

⑦ ★★★ Cathédrale de Notre-Dame. Wind your way to the eastern tip of the island to see the familiar silhouette of one of the world's most iconic cathedrals. Founded in 1160, Notre-Dame witnessed wars of religion and centuries of kings (Napoleon also crowned himself emperor here in 1804) before losing its riches to plunderers during the Revolution. By the 19th century, it had fallen into disrepair and was scheduled for demolition until author Victor Hugo, who wrote *The Hunchback of Notre-Dame,* led a successful campaign for its restoration.

Notre-Dame de Paris

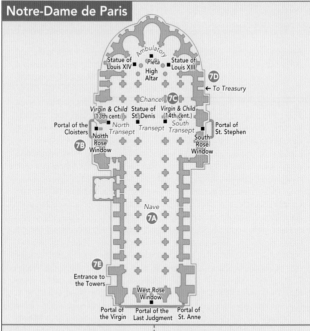

At the far end of the **7A** **nave** are three elaborately sculpted 13th-century portals: on the left, the Portal of the Virgin; in the center, the Portal of the Last Judgment; and on the right, the Portal of St. Anne. Above them all glow the ruby hues of the West Rose Window, its beauty surpassed only by the **7B** **North Rose Window.** The colors are especially vivid in the late afternoon.

The 12th-century Cathédrale de Notre-Dame.

Near the altar is the 14th-century **7C** **Virgin and Child.** In the **7D** **treasury,** you'll find a collection of crosses and ancient reliquaries, including the Crown of Thorns (brought from the Sainte-Chapelle). To get an up-close look at the cathedral's famous gargoyles, you must climb 67m (220 ft.) up the **7E** **tower** on old stone staircases—a strenuous workout, but the non-acrophobic will love the views of the fanciful and detailed hobgoblins, devils, and chimeras. ⏱ *1 hr. Parvis Notre-Dame/ Place Jean Paul II, 4th.* ☎ *01-42-34-56-10. www.cathedraledeparis.com. Free admission to cathedral, 8.50€ to towers, 3€ to treasury. Cathedral daily 8am–6:45pm. Towers Apr–Sept Mon–Fri 10am–6pm, Sat–Sun 10am–11pm; Jul–Aug daily 10am–11pm; Oct–Mar daily 10am–5:30pm. Treasury Mon–Sat 9:30am–6pm, Sun 2–6pm. Métro: Cité.*

8 ★ **La Fourmi Ailée.** Escape the crowds around Notre-Dame by crossing the pont au Double to the Left Bank. A 5-minute walk past Square René Viviani brings you to the "Flying Ant" tearoom, where sticky cakes and excellent hot dishes, such as veal blanquette (15€), are served in a library-like room. *8 rue du Fouarre, 5th.* ☎ *01-43-29-40-99. $.*

9 ★★ **Relaxing in Saint-Germain.** Head right as you leave the cafe and go up Rue Dante to join Boulevard Saint-Germain (turning right) and, after 5 minutes, the bustle of Saint-Germain-des-Prés. This area was the incubator for artistic creativity in the 1920s, for Nazi resistance in the 1940s, and for student revolution in the 1960s. These days, you can get a great cup of coffee, drop a wad of money on high-fashion clothes, or spend a night on the town. The best way to experience the neighborhood is to wander along glittering, tree-lined Boulevard Saint-Germain, soaking up the atmosphere and stopping at shops and bars that spark your fancy. The district is also the realm of Paris's historic literary cafes: the stylish **Café de Flore,** 172 bd. St-Germain (☎ 01-45-48-55-26), a favorite of the philosopher Jean-Paul Sartre; and the more touristy **Les Deux Magots,** 6 place St-Germain-des-Prés (☎ 01-45-48-55-26), a regular haunt of both Sartre and Hemingway. At either spot, you can linger over a *café* or enjoy a complete meal (at expensive prices), although for the cost of your drink or meal, you can stay at your table and people-watch as long as you like.

10 ★★ **Boat Tripping.** If you have any energy left after dinner, walk down to the riverside at the pont Neuf and catch one of Vedettes du Pont Neuf's long, low boats. By night, they glow with lights as they navigate the river, offering magical views of Paris. ① *1 hr. Square du Vert Galant, 4th.* ☎ *01-46-33-98-38. www.vedettes-dupontneuf.com. Tickets 13€ adults, 7€ children 4–12, free for children 3 & under. Mar–Oct daily 10:30am–10:30pm, about every 30 min.; Nov–Feb daily 10:30am–10pm, about every 45 min.*

Outside Les Deux Magots cafe on Boulevard Saint-Germain.

The Best **in Two Days**

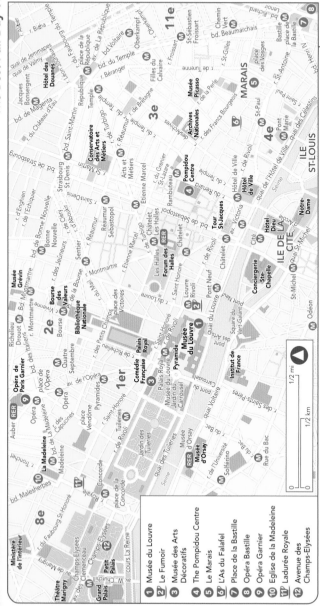

If you followed the 1-day tour of Paris, you've already had a good introduction to the city, but there's obviously lots more to see. Start your day early with a coffee and a fresh croissant—Café Marly, 93 rue de Rivoli, 1st, nestled underneath the Louvre's arches (☎ 01-49-26-06-60), is a good spot. START: **Métro to the Louvre.**

① ★★★ Musée du Louvre. Arrive early, or after 6pm on Wednesday or Friday (when the museum is open until 9:45pm), to catch the shortest lines at what is arguably the world's greatest art museum. The Louvre is so humongous you could easily spend a day in each wing and still not see everything. Overdosing on culture is best avoided by deciding what you want to see in advance. For help navigating the museum, opening times, and ticket prices, see the **Louvre tour** on p 30. ◷ *2 hr.*

② ★★ Le Fumoir. This handy cafe near the Louvre and Arts Décoratifs museums has a faithful following from Paris's literary and media crowds. Sink into a Chesterfield armchair and order a refreshing fruit cocktail, or fill up on salad, steak, or vegetarian risotto. *6 rue de l'amiral de Coligny, 1st.* ☎ *01-42-92-00-24. www.lefumoir.com. Métro: Louvre-Rivoli. $$$.*

③ ★ Musée des Arts Décoratifs. This excellent museum (set inside the Louvre palace but separate from the Louvre museum) contains one of the world's primary collections of design and decorative art. Sharing its space with the Musée de la Mode and the Musée de la Publicité (fashion and advertising museums both open for temporary exhibitions only), the museum's collection covers a breathtaking range of pieces, from medieval liturgical items, Art Nouveau and Art Deco furniture, Gothic paneling and Renaissance porcelain to 1970s psychedelic carpets, furniture by Philippe Starck, and furnishings from France's high-speed TGV trains. Ten period rooms show how the museum's collections would have looked in a real house. The most memorable are couturière Jeanne Lanvin's purple early Art Deco boudoir and a grandiose Louis-Philippe bedchamber. ◷ *1–1½ hrs. 107 rue de Rivoli, 1st.* ☎ *01-44-55-57-50. www.lesarts decoratifs.fr. Admission 9.50€ ages 26 & over, 8€ ages 18–25, free for children 17 & under & visitors 25 & under from E.U. countries. Tues–Wed & Fri–Sun 11am–6pm, Thurs 11am–9pm. Métro: Palais-Royal Musée du Louvre.*

The exoskeletal architecture of the Pompidou Centre.

METRO

④ ★★ The Pompidou Centre. If the Louvre's classic artworks leave you craving modernity, walk eastward, past the shops and cafes surrounding Châtelet-les-Halles, to Paris's most avant-garde building, the Pompidou Centre—one of the world's leading modern and contemporary art museums. Even by today's standards, the museum's bold, "exoskeletal" architecture, with brightly painted pipes, ducts, and escalator tubes crisscrossing on the outside, looks eccentric. *See p 42,* **①**.

⑤ ★★ The Marais. After so much culture, I find nothing more relaxing than strolling around the winding medieval streets of the Marais district—traditionally the city's old Jewish quarter and home to magnificent 17th- and 18th-century mansions (called *hôtels*). You can spend hours perusing its charming boutiques and tiny Jewish bakeries and absorbing museums if you take the Marais tour (p 60). One of its most picturesque squares is the Place des Vosges—Paris's oldest square, remarkable for its perfect symmetry, formed by 36 red-brick-and-stone arcades with sharply pitched roofs. In 1615, a 3-day party was held here celebrating Louis XIII's marriage to Anne of Austria. ① *2 hr. Most Jewish shops and restaurants close Fri evening through Sat, the Jewish Sabbath. Many boutiques open Sun. Métro: St-Paul.*

Falafel from Chez Hannah in the Marais.

⑥ ★ L'As du Falafel. This tiny cafe, with a window for takeout orders, makes (along with Chez Hannah down the same street, at no. 54) the best falafel sandwiches (from 5€) in the city. Unless it's raining, eat it on a bench in nearby Place des Vosges. (See previous stop.) *34 rue des Rosiers, 4th.* ☎ *01-48-87-63-60. $.*

⑦ ★ Place de la Bastille. From Place des Vosges, it's a very short walk to Place de la Bastille, the site of one of the most famous moments in French Revolutionary history. Here stood the Bastille prison, a massive building that loomed ominously over the city as a symbol of royal authority. On July 14, 1789, a mob attacked it, and its fall marked the beginning of the people's uprising that eventually led to the founding of the first French republic, in 1792. Today, the site is home to the modern Bastille Opera House and a busy traffic circle. The central column, the Colonne de Juillet, honors the casualties of the 1830 revolution, which ironically put Louis-Philippe on the throne after the upheaval of the Napoleonic wars. ① *15 min. Métro: Bastille.*

⑧ ★ Opéra Bastille. This impossible-to-miss behemoth, which opened in 1989, is the home of the Opéra National de Paris. It's clear that the designer of the building, Carlos Ott, paid a lot of attention to its appearance, but music lovers say it would have been nice if acoustics had been taken into consideration too. Despite this, operas played here are of the highest standard. Tickets are sold online, or you can try your luck 40 minutes before the performance, when remaining

tickets are sold off at a discount.
🕐 *15 min. 2 place de la Bastille, 4th.*
☎ *08-92-89-90-90 (0.34€/min.) or
33-1-73-60-26-26. www.operadeparis.
fr. Tickets 5€–130€. Métro: Bastille.*

⑨ ★★ Opéra Garnier. On your
second day (or third, if you followed
the 1-day tour), start by seeing what
opera used to look like in Paris:
Charles Garnier's architectural explosion goes beyond baroque and well
into the splendors of rococo. This
was the city's main opera house
until Opéra Bastille came along,
but now it also hosts dance performances beneath an elaborate ceiling painted by Marc Chagall in 1964.
The facade is all marble and flowing sculpture, with gilded busts and
multihued pillars. This is where the
Phantom did his haunting (a man-
made lake below the opera house
inspired novelist Gaston Leroux to
create his tragic antihero). Even if
you don't want to see a ballet, buy a
visitor's ticket (10€, 6€ ages 24 and
under) to admire the flamboyant
gilded interior, including the grand
staircase and the main theater (daily
10am–5pm; until 1pm on matinee
performance days). 🕐 *20 min. Place
de l'Opéra, 9th.* ☎ *08-92-89-90-90
(0.34€/min.) or 33-1-73-60-26-26.
www.operadeparis.fr. Tickets
5€–130€. Métro: Opéra.*

⑩ ★★ Eglise de la Madeleine.
Tear yourself away from the Art
Nouveau–style department stores
behind the opera house, on Boulevard Haussmann (**Galeries Lafayette** and **Au Printemps,** p 84), and
head west down Boulevard des
Capucines to this neoclassical
church, designed by Barthélémy
Vignon in 1806 as a "temple of
glory" for Napoleon Bonaparte. The
exterior, which mirrors the Assemblée Nationale on the other side of
Place de la Concorde, is marked by
fluted Corinthian columns, while
interior highlights

include a wonderful frieze of the
Last Judgment and a painting of
the history of Christianity by Jules-
Claude Ziegler. The square around
the church, **Place de la Madeleine,**
is a foodie paradise, with top-end
restaurants and such luxury food
shops as **Fauchon** (p 86). 🕐 *30min.
Place de la Madeleine, 8th.* ☎ *01-
44-51-69-00. www.eglise-lamadeleine.
com. Free admission. Daily 9:30am–
7pm. Métro: Madeleine.*

⑪ ★★★ Ladurée Royale. After
a long day traversing the city, tea
and cakes might be in order. The
19th-century dark wood, frescoed
ceilings, and gilded mirrors make
this one of the most atmospheric
tearooms in Paris. The macaroons
and pistachio pain-au-chocolats are
a dream. *16 rue Royale, 8th.* ☎ *01-42-
60-21-79. www.laduree.fr. Mon–Thurs
8:30am–7:30pm, Fri–Sat 8:30am–
8pm, Sun 10am–7pm. Métro: Made-
leine or Concorde. $$.*

**⑫ ★★ Avenue des Champs-
Elysées.** Although it's not as
beautiful as most of us imagine,
this 2km (1¼-mile) avenue—the
symbolic gathering place for
national parades and sports victory
celebrations, thanks to Napoleon's
early-19th-century **Arc de Triom-
phe** (p 24)—is inseparable from
Paris in the minds of most people.
It is also part of Paris's **Golden Tri-
angle** (along with av. Georges V
and av. Montaigne), where Chanel,
Louis Vuitton, and other designer
boutiques stand alongside lavish
palace hotels, such as the Hôtel
Georges V. You'll find plenty for
tighter budgets, too: Such mass-
market shops as H&M, Marks &
Spencer, and Zara line the sidewalk
along with cinemas, bars, the **Lido**
cabaret (p 131), and the famous
Queen nightclub (p 120).

The Best in Three Days

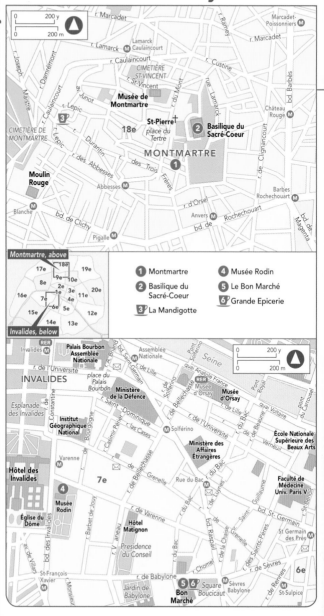

Montmartre, above

Invalides, below

1. Montmartre
2. Basilique du Sacré-Coeur
3. La Mandigotte
4. Musée Rodin
5. Le Bon Marché
6. Grande Epicerie

After a few days of sightseeing, you may want to slow down a bit. A good way of getting a leisurely feel for two very different parts of the city is to spend the morning amid the cobblestones and windmills of Montmartre before heading to the throng of boutiques in the Saint-Germain district, south of the Seine, in the afternoon. If you fancy slackening the pace even more, choose one of these two areas and follow the full-day tours on p 52 or p 64.

START: **Métro to Abesses or Place Blanche.**

❶ ★★★ **Montmartre.** With its steep hills, staircase streets, quaint windmills, and sweeping views, this is the most romantic neighborhood in Paris, and many would say the most beautiful. Unfortunately, it's not exactly a secret—prepare yourself for some tacky souvenir shops and the ever-present tourist onslaught around the Sacré Coeur. Still, spending a morning wandering around the streets of Montmartre is enough to make the heart flutter (and not just from the exertion of climbing all those stairs). Take the Métro to Abesses or Blanche and head upward. Fall in love with such streets as Rue des

The Basilica Sacré Coeur crowns the highest hill in Paris.

Abbesses, Rue des Trois Frères, or Rue des Martyrs. Find the windmills on Rue Lepic or the racier one atop the still-titillating Moulin Rouge on the boulevard below. For more guidance, try the Montmartre walking tour on p 64. ⏱ *2 hr. Métro: Abbesses or Place Blanche.*

❷ ★★★ **Sacré Coeur.** You can either take a funicular up from the end of Rue Berthe or, better still, wander to Sacré Coeur via the bustling Place du Tertre; however you get here, this white wedding-cake basilica will draw a gasp from you when it first hovers into view. Construction began in 1876 and didn't end until 1919—the whole thing was paid for by donations from the faithful to thank God for freeing Paris from the German invaders of the 1870–71 Franco-Prussian War. The mosaics inside—on the ceiling, walls, and floors—are almost dizzying, and the panoramic view from the steps out front is almost as splendid as the one from its dome, from where a panorama unfolds 50km (30 miles) into the distance. The Sacré Coeur's bell, called La Savoyarde, is 3m (10 ft.) wide and weighs 18,835 kg (19 tons), making it the biggest bell in France. ⏱ *1 hr. Place Saint-Pierre, 18th.* ☎ *01-53-41-89-00. www.sacre-coeur-montmartre.com. Free admission to basilica, 7€ to dome & crypt. Daily 6am–10:45pm (dome 9am–5:45pm). Métro: Abbesses.*

3 ★★ La Mandigotte. Back along Rue Lepic, tourist traps give way to pleasant bohemian eateries like this one, not far from the Café des Deux Moulins, where Amélie worked in the film of the same name. Dishes—think roast pork stuffed with apples—are fresh and copious, and the atmosphere is wholly Montmartrois. *68 rue Lepic, 18th.* ☎ *01-42-59-34-26. $.*

4 ★★ Musée Rodin. A short Métro ride will bring you to this peaceful museum, where the sculptor Auguste Rodin once had his studio. Today his works are scattered inside and outside a somber 18th-century mansion of gray stone. *The Thinker* perches pensively in the courtyard, while the lovers in *The Kiss* embrace in perpetuity inside. There's also a room devoted to the oft-overlooked works of Rodin's talented mistress, Camille Claudel. It's rarely crowded, so it's a good option when things are

The Thinker *in the courtyard of the Musée Rodin.*

overwhelming at the Louvre. ⏲ *1 hr. Hôtel Biron, 79 rue de Varenne, 7th.* ☎ *01-44-18-61-10. www.musee-rodin.fr. Admission 9€ ages 26 & over, 5€ ages 18–25, free for children 17 & under & visitors 25 & under from E.U. countries. Garden only 1€. Tues–Sun 10am–5:45pm. Métro: Varenne or Invalides. RER: Invalides.*

5 ★ Shopping at Le Bon Marché. If you haven't found everything you hoped to yet, and you're tired of walking from boutique to boutique, do what the locals do and come to this swank department store. If you fancy an extra treat, book the personalized shopping service at the "Conciergerie." You can even have a manicure or be guided through the "Theater of Beauty." The place is all very designer-label oriented, which may put some strains on the holiday budget. But this is Paris's oldest department store, and even the elevator is designer, so you should at least take a look. ⏲ *2 hr. 24 rue de Sèvres, 7th.* ☎ *01-44-39-80-00. www.lebonmarche.com. Mon–Sat 10am–8pm (Thurs–Fri until 9pm). Métro: Sèvres-Babylone.*

6 ★ Grande Epicerie. In a building connected to the Bon Marché, this grand food hall contains all the pâtés and cheeses your heart could desire. You can build yourself a gorgeous picnic, or take a seat in the excellent brasserie and let someone else do all the work. *38 rue de Sèvres, 7th.* ☎ *01-44-39-81-00. www.lagrandeepicerie.com. Mon–Sat 8:30am–9pm. $$.* ●

LE PENSEVR
DE RODIN OFFERT
PAR SOVSCRIPTION
PVBLIQVE AV PEVPLE

20

Monumental Paris

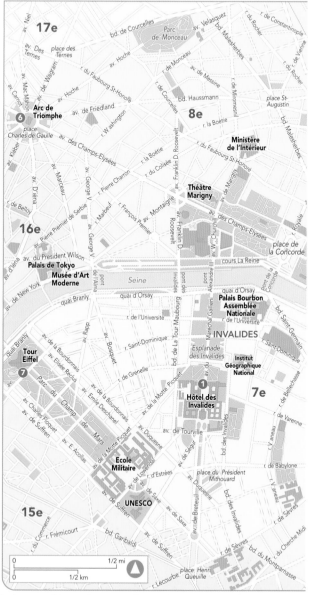

17e

av. Niel

bd. de Courcelles

Parc de Monceau

av. Velasquez

r. du Rocher

r. de Constantinople

av. Des Ternes

place des Ternes

av. Hoche

av. de Monceau

av. de Messine

bd. Malesherbes

r. de Vienne

r. du Rocher

av. de Wagram

r. du Faubourg St-Honoré

r. de Courcelles

bd. Haussmann

r. de Miromesnil

place St-Augustin

av. Mac Mahon

av. de Hoche

av. de Friedland

8e

r. la Boétie

av. Carnot

Arc de Triomphe ❻

av. des Champs-Elysées

r. W. Washington

r. la Boétie

r. du Faubourg St-Honoré

Ministère de l'Intérieur

bd. Malesherbes

place Charles de Gaulle

av. Kléber

r. Pierre Charron

r. du Colisée

r. Franklin D. Roosevelt

av. de Marigny

r. Royale

av. d'Iéna

av. Marceau

r. George V

r. Marbeuf

av. Montaigne

Théâtre Marigny

16e

av. Pierre Premier de Serbie

r. François Premier

av. des Champs-Elysées

place de la Concorde

de Belloy

r. George V

av. Franklin D. Roosevelt

av. W. Churchill

cours La Reine

av. d'Iéna

av. du President Wilson

Palais de Tokyo
Musée d'Art Moderne

pont de l'Alma

Seine

pont des Invalides

pont Alexandre III

quai d'Orsay

pont de la Concorde

av. de New York

quai Branly

quai d'Orsay

Palais Bourbon Assemblée Nationale

bd. Saint-Germain

r. de l'Université

r. de l'Université

av. Rapp

r. Saint-Dominique

av. Maréchal Gallieni

INVALIDES

r. Saint-Dominique

Tour Eiffel ❼

quai Branly

av. de la Bourdonnais

av. Elisée Reclus

av. Bosquet

bd. de La Tour Maubourg

Esplanade des Invalides

Institut Géographique National

r. de Bellechasse

Parc du

av. de la Bourdonnais

r. de Grenelle

❶

7e

av. Charles Floquet

Champ

av. Emile Deschanel

Hôtel des Invalides

r. de Varenne

av. de Suffren

de

Mars

av. de la Motte Picquet

av. de Tourville

r. Vaneau

av. E. Acollas

av. Duquesne

Ecole Militaire

av. de Ségur

bd. des Invalides

place du Président Mithouard

r. de Babylone

15e

av. de Lowendal

d'Estrées

av. de Saxe

av. Duquesne

r. Vaneau

r. de Sèvres

r. du Commerce

r. Frémicourt

av. de Suffren

UNESCO

av. de Saxe

av. de Breteuil

bd. des Invalides

bd. de Sèvres

r. du Cherche Midi

bd. Garibaldi

r. de Sèvres

bd. du Montparnasse

| 0 | | 1/2 mi |
| 0 | | 1/2 km |

place Henri Queuille

r. Lecourbe

Previous page: Clément Ader's Victorian flying machine at the Musée des Arts et Métiers.

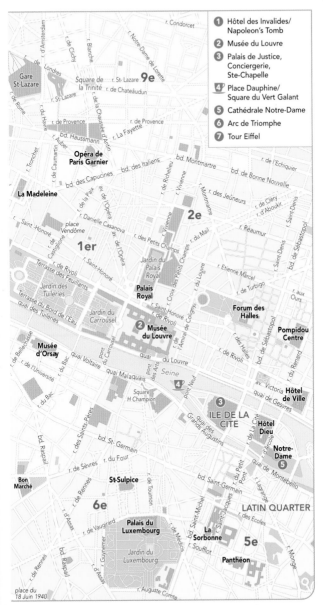

1. Hôtel des Invalides/Napoleon's Tomb
2. Musée du Louvre
3. Palais de Justice, Conciergerie, Ste-Chapelle
4. Place Dauphine/Square du Vert Galant
5. Cathédrale Notre-Dame
6. Arc de Triomphe
7. Tour Eiffel

This tour covers a lot of ground, so be prepared for a busy day. For your efforts, you'll see the city's most glorious edifices all at one go. If you get an early start and keep moving, you should be able to make it to the Eiffel Tower (the last stop) by sunset. START: **Métro to Invalides.**

① ★★★ **Hôtel des Invalides/ Napoleon's Tomb.** The imposing Les Invalides complex, with its symmetrical corridors and beautiful Dôme church (Libéral Bruand and Jules Hardouin-Mansart's golden-domed masterpiece), was built in 1670 by Louis XIV as a military hospital and a showpiece of the Sun King's military power. Approach it from the cherub-clad pont Alexandre III to see it as intended, from the end of its perfectly balanced gardens, lined with canons. Inside, along with accouterments of Napoleon's life and death, is the Musée de l'Armée, with enough historic weaponry (vicious battle-axes, clumsy blunderbusses) to mount another revolution. Among the collection's gems are suits of armor worn by the kings and dignitaries of France, including one worn by Louis XIV and François I's "armor suit of the lion." Henri II ordered his suit engraved with the monograms of both his mistress, Diane de Poitiers, and his wife, Catherine de Médicis. The complex also contains the Historical Charles de Gaulle, a high-tech audiovisual monument covering the whole of de Gaulle's life, particularly his role in World War II; the Musée des Plans Reliefs, the collection of scale-model cities Vauban, Louis XIV's military engineer, used for planning military attacks; and of course, Napoleon's tomb. Set inside the Dôme church, his over-the-top tomb features giant statues that represent his victories surrounding his famously tiny body. You can also see his death mask and an oil painting by Paul Delaroche, painted at the time of Napoleon's first banishment, in 1814. ⏱ *1 hr. 129 rue de Grenelle, 7th.* ☎ *01-42-44-38-77. www.invalides. org. Admission 9.50€ ages 26 & over, 7.50€ ages 18–25, free for children 17 & under & visitors 25 & under from E.U. countries. Oct–Mar daily 10am–5pm; Apr–May & Sept daily 10am–6pm. Oct–June closed 1st Mon of the month. Historical Charles de Gaulle closed Mon. Métro: Invalides.*

② ★★★ **Musée du Louvre.** The home of da Vinci's *Mona Lisa* is one of the world's largest and best museums, set in Paris's former royal palace. It's worth spending a day here (see "Exploring the Louvre,"

A view of the Sun King's Hôtel des Invalides (right) and the Eiffel Tower.

The Musée du Louvre, viewed through I.M. Pei's glass pyramid in the courtyard.

p 30), but for this tour, admire it from the outside. ⏱ *20 min.*

➌ ★★★ Palais de Justice, Conciergerie & Sainte-Chapelle.

Take the pont Neuf to the Île de la Cité. Turn left after you cross the bridge, and you'll see the complex made up of the Palais de Justice (law courts), the Conciergerie (formerly a prison, now a museum), and the exquisite Sainte-Chapelle church. The Palais is still the center of the French judicial system, and it's worth a peek inside at its grand lobby. Once a palace, the Conciergerie was converted to a prison during the Revolution and became a symbol of terror—Paris's answer to the Tower of London. Carts once frequently pulled up to the Conciergerie to haul off fresh victims for the guillotine. Among the few imprisoned here who lived to tell the tale was American political theorist and writer Thomas Paine. Inside, you can learn about the bloody history of the Conciergerie and visit some of the old prison cells, including a re-creation of Marie Antoinette's. The Sainte-Chapelle—stunning in afternoon light—was built in the 13th century to hold a crown of thorns that King Louis IX believed Christ wore during his crucifixion (it's now in Notre-Dame). The chapel's 15 stained-glass windows comprise more than 1,000 scenes depicting the Christian story from the Garden of Eden through to the Apocalypse, shown on the great Rose Window. (Read them from bottom to top and from left to right.) The stained glass of Sainte-Chapelle is magnificent in daylight, glowing with reds that have inspired the saying "wine the color of Sainte-Chapelle's windows." ⏱ *1 hr. 2–6 bd. du Palais, 1st.* ☎ *01-53-40-60-80. http://conciergerie.monuments-nationaux.fr. Free admission to Palais de Justice; Conciergerie 8.50€ ages 26 & over, 5.50€ ages 18–25, free for ages 17 & under & visitors 25 & under from E.U. countries; Sainte-Chapelle 8.50€ ages 26 & over, 5.50€ ages 18–25, free for children 17 & under & visitors 25 & under 26 from E.U. countries. Combined ticket for Conciergerie & Sainte-Chapelle 13€; concessions 8.50€ & free entry, as above. Daily 9:30am–6pm. Métro: Cité.*

➍ ★ Place Dauphine/Square du Vert Gallant.

Place Dauphine, where the pont Neuf crosses the island, has several decent restaurants and cafes. If you've brought a picnic lunch, go to the Square du Vert Gallant opposite, at the tip of the island, and spread out on the grass or near the water's edge to eat with a view of the Louvre. *$–$$.*

⑤ ★★★ Cathédrale Notre-Dame. For a good view of the buttresses, take the short bridge—pont de l'Archevêché—just behind the cathedral to Île Saint-Louis. ① *1 hr. See p 26,* ⑦.

⑥ ★★★ Arc de Triomphe. The world's largest triumphal arch was commissioned by Napoleon in 1806 to commemorate the victories of his Grande Armée. The monument is engraved with the names of hundreds of generals (those underlined died in battle) who commanded French troops in Napoleonic victories. The arch was finished in 1836, after Napoleon's death. His remains, brought from St. Helena in 1840, passed under it on the journey to his final resting place at the Hôtel des Invalides. These days, the arch is the focal point of state funerals and the site of the Tomb of the Unknown Soldier, in whose honor an eternal flame burns. It's also a huge traffic circle, representing certain death to pedestrians, so you reach the arch via an underground passage (well signposted). The constant roar of traffic can ruin the mood, but the view from the top (accessible via elevator or stairs) makes enduring the din worthwhile. The last leg of your tour is a 20-minute walk away. You can also hop back on the Métro to Trocadéro or flag down a taxi on the Champs Elysées. ① *45 min. The Arc de Triomphe is open late at night, so if you prefer a nighttime view, you can put this off until after dinner. Place Charles de Gaulle–Etoile, 8th.* ☎ *01-55-37-73-77. www.arc-de-triomphe.monuments-nation-aux.fr. Admission 9.50€ ages 26 & over, 6€ ages 18–25, free for children 17 & under & visitors 25 & under from E.U. countries. Apr–Sept daily 10am–11pm; Oct–Mar daily 10am–10:30pm. Métro/RER: Charles de Gaulle–Etoile.*

⑦ ★★★ Tour Eiffel. At last. It's the Eiffel Tower to English speakers and the *Tour Eiffel* to the rest of the world, but whatever you call it, it is synonymous with Paris. The tower was meant to be temporary, built by Gustave-Alexandre Eiffel

A subterranean passage undercuts traffic, leading pedestrians safely to the Arc de Triomphe.

A view of the Eiffel Tower from the carousel in the Luxembourg Gardens.

(who also created the framework for the Statue of Liberty) in 1889 for the Universal Exhibition. It weighs 7,000 tons but exerts about the same pressure on the ground as an average-size person sitting in a chair. Praised by some and denounced by others, the tower created as much controversy in the 1880s as I.M. Pei's glass pyramid at the Louvre did in the 1980s. The tower, including its TV antenna, is 317m (1,040 ft.) high, and from the top you can see for 65km (40 miles). But the view of the tower is just as important as the view from it. If you go to Trocadéro on the Métro and then walk from the Palais de Chaillot gardens across the Seine, you'll get the best view (not to mention photo opportunities). I always come right at sunset or just after dark. Inside the tower's lacy ironwork are restaurants, bars, and historic memorabilia. Take your time, have a drink, or even book a table at Alain Ducasse's pricey restaurant **Le Jules Verne** (reserve 3 months in

advance for an evening meal; ☎ 01-45-55-61-44), and enjoy sweeping views from the second level as you dine. If your pockets aren't that deep, his brasserie Altitude 95, on the first floor, is an excellent compromise. Or opt for a glass of bubbly from the tiny top floor champagne bar—no more than a barman behind a hatch. ⏱ *2 hr. Champ de Mars, 7th.* ☎ *01-44-11-23-23. www.tour-eiffel.fr. Admission lift to 1st or 2nd floor 8.50€ adults, 7€ ages 12–24, 4€ ages 3–11; lift to top floor 15€ adults, 13€ ages 12–24, 10€ ages 3–11; stairs to 1st and 2nd floors 5€ adults, 3.50€ ages 12–24, 3€ ages 3–11, free for children 2 & under. Open by lift Jan to mid-June & Sept 2–Dec daily 9:30am–11:45pm; mid-June to Sept 1 daily 9am–12:45am. By stairs Jan to mid-June & Sept 2–Dec daily 9:30am–6:30pm; mid-June to Sept 1 daily 9am–12:45am. Métro: Trocadéro, Ecole Militaire, or Bir-Hakeim. RER: Champs-de-Mars-Tour-Eiffel.*

Paris with Kids

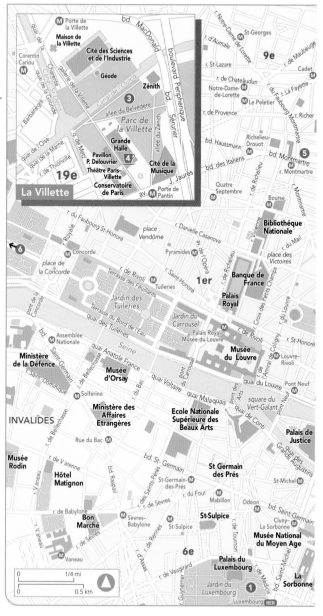

La Villette

- Porte de la Villette M
- Maison de la Villette
- Cité des Sciences et de l'Industrie
- Géode
- Zénith
- Parc de la Villette
- Grande Halle
- Pavillon P. Delouvrier
- Théâtre Paris–Villette
- Cité de la Musique
- Conservatoire de Paris
- Porte de Pantin M

9e

Bibliothèque Nationale

1er

Banque de France

Palais Royal

Musée du Louvre

place de la Concorde

Jardin des Tuileries

Ministère de la Défence

Musée d'Orsay

Ministère des Affaires Etrangères

INVALIDES

Ecole Nationale Supérieure des Beaux Arts

Palais de Justice

Musée Rodin

Hôtel Matignon

St Germain des Prés

Bon Marché

St-Sulpice

Musée National du Moyen Age

6e

Palais du Luxembourg

La Sorbonne

Jardin du Luxembourg

Luxembourg RER

0   1/4 mi
0   0.5 km

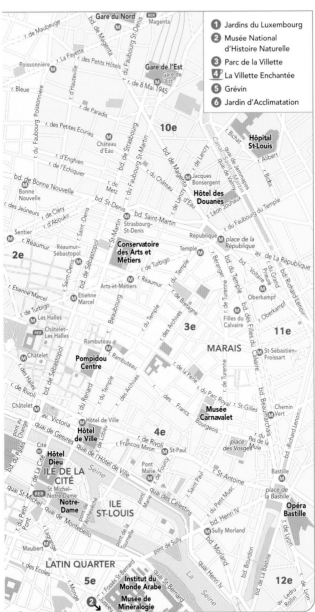

1. Jardins du Luxembourg
2. Musée National d'Histoire Naturelle
3. Parc de la Villette
4. La Villette Enchantée
5. Grévin
6. Jardin d'Acclimatation

Let's face it: Most kid-approved attractions are outdoors, which means you're dangerously reliant on good weather. But this tour has been designed to keep them smiling come rain or shine. Yet even the best-laid plans fail—in which case you can rush them off for a day at Disneyland Paris (p 158). START: **Métro to Odéon.**

A merry-go-round in the Jardins du Luxembourg.

① Jardins du Luxembourg.

Kids can run amok in these elegant gardens, which are done in classic French style, with urns and statuary and trees planted in patterns. Statues peek out everywhere as children sail toy boats on the ponds, ride the ponies, or catch a puppet show, if you get lucky with timing. Kids can also watch the locals play *boules* (lawn bowling), but are unlikely to be invited to join in. Don't miss the ornate, evocative Fountaines de Medicis, in the northeast corner of the park. ⏱ *1 hr. Métro: Odéon. RER: Luxembourg.*

② Musée National d'Histoire Naturelle.

The giant whale skeleton hanging just inside the front door of this natural history museum lets you know right off the bat that the kids are going to be fine here. Beyond those bones in the Galerie de l'Evolution are more skeletons of dinosaurs and mastodons, and galleries filled with sparkling minerals and rare plants. In the surrounding gardens (the Jardin des Plantes), there's also a wonderful menagerie with small animals in simulated natural habitats. A good place to linger if the weather turns gray. ⏱ *90 min. 56 rue Cuvier, 5th.* ☎ *01-40-79-54-79. www.mnhn.fr. Admission 7€ adults, 5€ ages 4–16, free for children 3 & under (1 full-price ticket gives reduced price access to the Menagerie). Wed–Fri & Mon 10am–5pm, Sat–Sun 10am–6pm. Métro: Jussieu or Gare d'Austerlitz.*

La Cité des Sciences children's museum in the Parc de la Villette.

Bumper cars in the Jardin d'Acclimatation.

❸ ★★★ Parc de la Villette. Take the Métro to Jaurès or Stalingrad and then stroll or bike along the redeveloped Canal de l'Ourcq to Parc de la Villette, a retro-futurist succession of gardens for kids to run around in. There's an IMAX cinema at 26 av. Corentin-Cariou (☎ 08-92-70-08-40, 0.34€/min.; admission 11€ adults, 9€ 25 and under; www.lageode.fr; Métro: Porte de la Villette) and a fabulous children's science museum, La Cité des Sciences, at 30 av. Corentin-Cariou (☎ 01-40-05-70-00; www.cite-sciences.fr; admission 11€ adults, 9€ ages 7–25, free for children under 6; Métro: Porte de la Villette). See p 71, ❺ for a fuller list of attractions. ⏱ *3 hr. 19th.*

❹ ★ La Villette Enchantée. If your family needs refreshments in the park, La Villette Enchantée is a children-friendly cafe with a terrace that rolls out onto the lawn; ideal for letting your brood run around while you relax over coffee. *211 av. Jean Jaurès, 19th.* ☎ *01-40-03-75-75. www.lavilletteenchantee.fr. Métro: Porte de la Villette.* $.

❺ Grévin. If the weather is bad, make this your last stop of the day. If it's good, skip this stop and go on to the next one. At this waxworks museum, kids will enjoy wandering among stars—both American (Madonna) and international (soccer star Zinédine Zidane). Among the 300 wax figures, you'll find heads of state, artists, writers, and historical figures—at times, the museum even verges on educational. ⏱ *1 hr. 10 bd. Montmartre, 9th.* ☎ *01-47-70-85-05. www.grevin.com. Admission 23€ adults 15 & up, 16€ children 7–14, free for children 6 & under. Mon–Fri 10am–6:30pm, Sat–Sun 10am–7pm. Closed 1st week in Oct. Métro: Grands-Boulevards.*

❻ ★★ Jardin d'Acclimatation. Let the kids while away the rest of a sunny afternoon here. You can start with a ride on a green-and-yellow narrow-gauge train from porte Maillot to the entrance (every 30 min. Wed and Sat–Sun). Along the way, there's a house of mirrors, an archery range, miniature golf, a small (and vaguely worrying) zoo, a bowling alley, a puppet theater, playgrounds, kid-size rides, shooting galleries, and food stalls. Kids can ride ponies and paddle about in boats—they can even drive little cars. Bear in mind that it's only for little ones; teenagers will hate it. ⏱ *2–3 hr. Bois de Boulogne, 16th.* ☎ *01-40-67-90-82. www.jardindacclimatation.fr. Admission 3€ to enter (then 2.90€ for each attraction, or 35€ for 15 rides), free for children 3 and under. June–Sept daily 10am–7pm; Oct–May daily 10am–6pm. Métro: Sablons or Porte Maillot.*

Exploring the Louvre

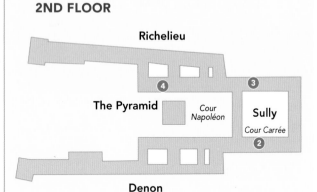

2ND FLOOR

Richelieu

The Pyramid

Cour Napoléon

Sully

Cour Carrée

Denon

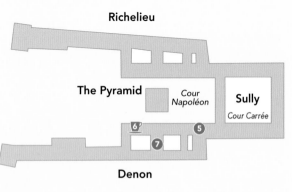

1ST FLOOR

Richelieu

The Pyramid

Cour Napoléon

Sully

Cour Carrée

Denon

1. *Venus de Milo*
2. *The Turkish Bath*
3. *The Card Sharper*
4. *The Lacemaker*
5. *Winged Victory of Samothrace*
6. Café Mollien
7. *Mona Lisa*
8. Italian Sculpture
9. Islamic Art

GROUND FLOOR

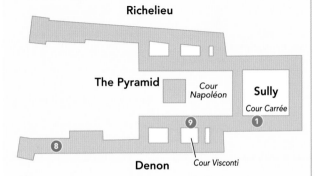

Richelieu

The Pyramid

Cour Napoléon

Sully

Cour Carrée

1

9

8

Denon

Cour Visconti

THE PYRAMID

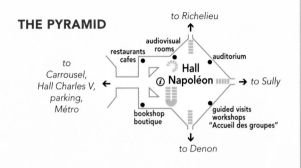

to Richelieu

audiovisual rooms

restaurants cafes

auditorium

Hall Napoléon

to Carrousel, Hall Charles V, parking, Métro

to Sully

bookshop boutique

guided visits workshops "Accueil des groupes"

to Denon

Before becoming a museum, the Musée du Louvre was France's main royal palace. In 1527, François I demolished most of the old castle to build a new one, which makes up part of the building you see today. (François also inadvertently founded part of the museum's collection—the *Mona Lisa* and *Virgin of the Rocks* once hung in his bathroom.) The rest of the building was completed over the centuries, particularly by Henri II and Napoleon. More recent additions include the glass pyramids designed by I.M. Pei (in 1989) and the brand-new Cour Visconti extension, which houses a wonderful Islamic art collection. START: **Métro to Palais Royal–Musée du Louvre.**

Travel Tip

Laid out end to end, the Louvre would be the size of several football fields, so put aside at least 3 to 4 hours to get a general feel for the place and browse a bit between stops. Pick up a map when you arrive at the museum and use it to find my suggested selection of works—the floor and rooms are marked for each entry.

① ★★★ **Venus de Milo.** Begin your tour in Greek Antiquities, where *Venus* stands alluringly, her drapery about to fall to the floor. The statue dates to 100 B.C. Myths about her abound—one story maintains that her arms were knocked off when she was hustled onto a French ship. Another claims she was rescued from a pottery kiln. Both are untrue—she was found buried as you see her now, along with part of an arm, a hand holding an apple, and a pair of small columns, one of which fit neatly into her base and bore the inscription ALEXANDROS, SON OF MENIDES, CITIZEN OF ANTIOCH, MADE THIS STATUE. Sadly, those parts were all lost over time. *Ground floor, Room 16.*

② ★ **The Turkish Bath.** Take the stairs to the second floor (if you're from the USA, remember that the French second floor is your third floor), where you'll see the titillating lush nudity of Jean-Auguste-Dominique Ingres's *The Turkish Bath.* Ingres was a popular French painter in the early 19th century, and this erotic idealized painting of overly friendly women lounging in a (very crowded) bath

The Musée du Louvre stretches almost a kilometer.

After all these millennia, Venus de Milo *still manages to work the crowd.*

was the masterwork of his final years. *2nd floor, Room 60.*

❸ ★★ **The Card Sharper.** In Room 24, you'll find Georges de la Tour's sensational *Tricheur (The Card Sharper),* painted around 1630. In this gorgeous work, complex relationships play out in shimmering colors. In the center, a courtesan holds her hand out for a glass of wine poured by a servant. Her cheating friend holds cards behind his back as she casts a colluding glance at him. The chubby-cheeked youth in the embroidered shirt is the victim of a plot. A cruel tale, playfully told. *2nd floor, Room 24.*

❹ ★★★ **The Lacemaker.** *The Lacemaker* (around 1664) is one of Johannes Vermeer's most famous paintings. It shows a young woman bent over her work, her shape forming a subtle pyramid, and her face, hair, and rich yellow blouse aglow. The book in the foreground is probably the Bible and sets the moral and religious tone of the painting. Vermeer's unique use of color and light are exemplified in

this work, which is usually surrounded by a crowd of admirers. *2nd floor, Room 38.*

❺ ★ **Winged Victory of Samothrace.** Head toward the Denon Wing, where at the top of the Daru stairs stands Nike, the goddess of victory, her wings flung back in takeoff, and the fabric of her skirts swirling around her, as fine as silk. The statue's origins are uncertain. Most scholars date it to somewhere between 220 and 190 B.C. The statue was discovered on the Greek island of Samothrace in 1863, and its base was discovered in 1879. In 1950, one of the statue's hands was found; it's on display in a glass case near the statue. An inscription on the statue's base includes the word RHODHIOS (Rhodes) and this, along with the fact that the statue stands on the prow of a ship, has led some scholars to theorize that the piece was commissioned in celebration of a naval victory by Rhodes. Others believe it was an offering made by a Macedonian general after a victory in Cyprus. Regardless of its origins,

The Winged Victory of Samothrace.

this glorious work is considered one of the best surviving Greek sculptures from that period. *Top of the Daru staircase.*

6 ★ **Café Mollien.** Ready for a break? Café Mollien is particularly enjoyable in the summertime, when the outdoor terrace is open. The café au lait is good here, as is the fresh smoked-salmon sandwich. *$.*

7 ★★★ ***Mona Lisa.*** It's a long way to the end of the Denon Wing and the hiding place of one of the world's most famous paintings, but everybody makes the trip. The enigmatic smile, the challenging eyes, the endless debates (Was she the wife of an Italian city official? Is she meant to be in mourning? Is "she" a man—perhaps even a self-portrait of da Vinci himself?) continue now as ever. The painting has been through a lot over the years. It was stolen in 1911 (by a Louvre employee who simply put the painting under his coat and walked out with it) and wasn't recovered until 1913. During World War II, it was housed in various parts of France for safekeeping. In 1956, the painting was severely damaged

after someone threw acid on it. In 1962 and 1963, it toured the United States, and was shown in New York City and Washington, D.C. In 1974, it was shown in Tokyo and Moscow. All the hype and history aside, some find actually seeing Leonardo da Vinci's *Mona Lisa* (painted between 1503 and 1507) a disappointment. It's a very small painting to have caused such a fuss and has been kept behind glass since it was slashed by a vandal in the 1990s. That, along with the crowds surrounding it, makes it difficult to connect with. Despite these shortcomings, few come to the Louvre without stopping by at least once. *1st floor, Room 6.*

8 ★★★ **Italian Sculpture.** Make your way down to the ground floor of the Denon Wing and head to Room 4, which is filled with exquisite Italian sculptures. Michelangelo's two statues are among the most dramatic in the room—the muscular arms of his *Rebellious Slave* are tensed furiously against his bindings, while the *Dying Slave* seems resigned to his fate. Both were commissioned in 1505 by Pope Julius II as funerary art. Look across the room for the delicate wings of Cupid, who clutches the

The Louvre: Practical Matters

The main entrances to the **Musée du Louvre,** 1st (☎ 01-40-20-53-17; www.louvre.fr) are at 99 rue de Rivoli, inside the Carousel du Louvre underground shopping mall, and the glass pyramid in the main courtyard. Tickets can be bought inside the museum, but expect a long line. To jump the queues, use the automatic ticket machines inside the Carousel du Louvre (just after the entrance at 99 rue de Rivoli) or buy them in advance at a FNAC (p 88) or online (www.ticketweb.com if you're from the United States or Canada, or www.louvre.fnacspectacles.com or www.ticketnet.fr if you're not), then go to the Passage Richelieu entrance, 93 rue de Rivoli.

To beat the crowds, arrive shortly after opening or after 6pm Wed or Fri. Admission is 11€, free for children 17 and under and visitors 25 and under from E.U. countries, and free for everyone the first Sunday of the month. Hours are Wednesday and Friday 9am to 9:45pm, Thursday and Saturday to Monday 9am to 6pm. Métro: Palais Royal–Musée du Louvre and Louvre Rivoli.

breast of Psyche in a pas de deux in pure white marble in Antonio Canova's *Cupid Awakening Psyche* (1793). It is love carved in stone. *Ground floor, Room 4.*

➒ ★★★ Cour Visconti.
Opened in 2012, the newly refurbished Cour Visconti section provides the Louvre's more than 2,000 pieces of Islamic art with an appropriately prominent setting. The fascinating collections (including many lavish pieces made for heads of state) highlight the development of Islamic art from its beginnings in the 7th century up until the early 19th, showing the differences in artistic styles according to culture, geography, and era.

The Mona Lisa *once hung over François I's bathtub.*

Paris for Museum Lovers

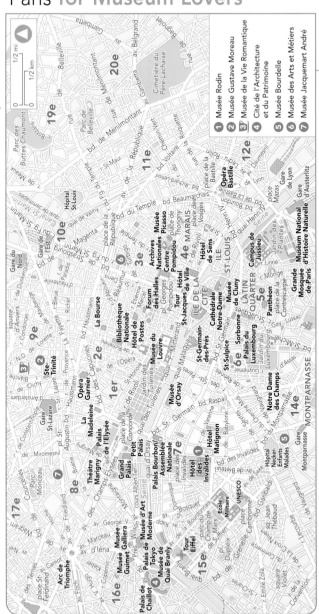

1 Musée Rodin
2 Musée Gustave Moreau
3 Musée de la Vie Romantique
3R Cité de l'Architecture et du Patrimoine
5 Musée Bourdelle
6 Musée des Arts et Métiers
7 Musée Jacquemart André

You'd need a lifetime to fully explore the hundreds of museums in Paris. Once you've visited the behemoths (the Louvre, Musée d'Orsay, and Centre Pompidou), there are dozens of beautiful, more intimate addresses dedicated to sculpture, inventions, and architecture. This section is not a tour per se, but a list to be dipped into as you please. START: **Métro to Varennes.**

The spiral staircase at the Musée Gustave Moreau.

Save on Admission Fees

All of Paris's municipal museums are free (see www.paris.fr for a full list). If you plan to visit several non-municipal museums over 2, 4, or 6 days, you'll save money with the Paris Museum Pass (www.parismuseumpass.com; 2 days 39€, 4 days 54€, 6 days 69€), available for purchase at more than 60 participating museums and online.

① ★★ **Musée Rodin.** This peaceful museum, housed in the building that was once sculptor Auguste Rodin's studio, can't help but inspire thoughts of romance. *The Thinker* ponders in the sublime gardens, while the lovers in *The Kiss* are locked in a permanent embrace inside. ① *1 hr. Hôtel Biron, 79 rue de Varenne, 7th.*

☎ 01-44-18-61-10. www.musee-rodin.fr. Admission museum 9€ ages 26 and& over, 5€ ages 18–25, free for children 17 & under & visitors 25 & under from E.U. countries; gardens 1€. Tues–Sun 10am–5:45pm. Métro: Varenne or Invaldies. RER: Invaldies.

② ★★ **Musée Gustave Moreau.** Painter Gustave Moreau was around at the same time as the Impressionists, but he worked against the prevailing mood, drawing inspiration from the Bible, Greek mythology, Leonardo da Vinci, and Indian miniatures. This atmospheric museum, where he lived and worked, reveals Moreau's obsession for knickknacks and furniture, which are displayed alongside his fabulous mythical beasts and fantasy worlds. ① *1 hr. 14 rue de la Rochefoucauld,*

9th. ☎ 01-48-74-38-50. www.musee-moreau.fr. Admission 5€ adults, 3€ ages 18–25, free for ages 17 & under, free for everyone 1st Sun of the month. Wed–Mon 10am–12:45pm & 2–5:15pm. Métro: Trinité.

3 ★★★ **Musée de la Vie Romantique.** Hidden from the rest of the world is this charming, green-shuttered 18th-century mansion that once housed composers Gioachino Rossini and Frédéric Chopin, novelist George Sand, and painter Eugène Delacroix. It takes the gâteau (cake), quite literally, in the rose garden, which doubles as an outside tearoom. Decadence is yours for the price of your café and tarte au citron (lemon tart). 16 rue Chaptal, 9th. ☎ 01-55-31-95-67. www.paris.fr. Tues–Sun 10am–6pm. Free admission. Métro: Pigalle, St-Georges, or Blanche.

4 kids ★★ **Cité de l'Architecture et du Patrimoine.** Comprising 8 sq. km (3 sq. miles) of space in the east wing of the Palais de Chaillot, the City of

Architecture and Heritage contains more than 850 breathtaking full-size copies of French architectural treasures, including molded portions of churches, châteaux, and great French cathedrals, such as Chartres. There are also reconstructions of modern architecture, the centerpiece of which is an apartment by Le Corbusier. ⏱ 2 hr. Palais de Chaillot, 1 place du Trocadéro, 16th. ☎ 01-58-51-52-00. www.citechaillot.fr. Admission 8€ adults, 5€ ages 19–25, free for ages 18 & under & visitors 25 & under from E.U. countries, free for everyone 1st Sun of the month. Wed & Fri–Mon 11am–7pm, Thurs 11am–9pm. Métro: Trocadéro.

5 ★★ **Musée Bourdelle.** Hidden away from the hustle and bustle of Montparnasse is the workshop where Rodin's star pupil, sculptor Antoine Bourdelle (1861–1929), lived and worked. The sumptuous array of statues, many inspired by Greek mythology, includes Centaure Mourant (The Dying Centaur) writhing in agony; Penelope, Ulysses's wife, who waited 20 years for her husband to return; and, in the gorgeous walled

An elaborate ceiling at the Cité de l'Architecture et du Patrimoine in the Palais de Chaillot.

The Musée Bourdelle in Montparnasse.

garden, the colossal General Alvear horse statue (part of an allegorical monument that was never finished). ⓘ *90 min. 16–18 rue Antoine-Bourdelle, 15th. ☎ 01-49-54-73-73. www.bourdelle.paris.fr. Free admission. Tues–Sun 10am–6pm. Closed public holidays. Métro: Montparnasse-Bienvenue.*

❻ kids **★★★ Musée des Arts et Métiers.** This museum, founded in the 18th century by Abbot Grégoire as "a store for useful new inventions," is an absolute gem. Housed in the former Benedictine church and priory of Saint-Martin-des-Champs, it exhibits some of the world's greatest inventions, from Pascal's calculating devices and celestial spheres to the first computers, steam-powered vehicles, and even airplanes (including the monoplane Louis Blériot flew across the English Channel in 1909). ⓘ *2 hr. 60 rue Réamur, 3rd. ☎ 01-53-01-82-00. www.arts-et-metiers.net. Admission 6.50€ adults, 4.50€ ages 18–25, free for ages 17 &*

under. Tues–Wed & Fri–Sun 10am–6pm, Thurs 10am–9:30pm. Métro: Arts et Métiers.

❼ kids **★★ Musée Jacquemart-André.** This decorative-arts museum, set in the stately former home of the collectors it's named for—Nélie Jacquemart and Edouard André—houses an array of rare 18th-century French paintings and furnishings, 17th-century Dutch and Flemish paintings, and Italian Renaissance works fit for a king. The salons drip with gilt and the ultimate in fin-de-siècle style. Works by Bellini, Carpaccio, Uccello, van Dyck, Rembrandt, Tiepolo, Rubens, Watteau, Boucher, Fragonard, and Mantegna hang on almost every wall. If you fancy a decadent snack, Mme. Jacquemart's high-ceilinged tearoom complies, with delicious sticky cakes and piping-hot tea (served 11:45am–5:30pm). ⓘ *1 hr. 158 bd. Haussmann, 8th. ☎ 01-45-62-11-59. www.musee-jacquemart-andre.com. Admission 11€ adults, 9.50€ ages 7–17, free for children 6 & under. Daily 10am–6pm. Métro: Miromesnil or St-Philippe du Roule.*

A sumptuous salon in the Musée Jacquemart-André.

Paris's Best Modern Art

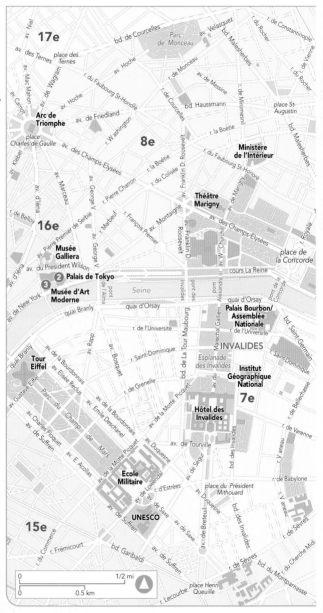

17e

bd. de Courcelles

Parc de Monceau

av. Velasquez

r. de Constantinople

r. du Rocher

r. de Vienne

r. du Rocher

av. des Ternes

place des Ternes

av. Hoche

av. de Monceau

r. de Messine

av. de Mac Mahon

av. du Faubourg St-Honoré

r. de Courcelles

bd. Haussmann

r. de Miromesnil

place St-Augustin

bd. Malesherbes

Arc de Triomphe

av. de Friedland

8e

av. de Wagram

av. Hoche

W. Washington

r. la Boétie

r. du Faubourg St-Honoré

Ministère de l'Intérieur

place Charles de Gaulle

av. des Champs-Elysées

r. la Boétie

r. du Colisée

Franklin D. Roosevelt

av. Kléber

16e

av. Marceau

av. George V

r. Pierre Charron

r. François Premier

Théâtre Marigny

av. de Marigny

r. Royale

r. de Belloy

av. Pierre Premier de Serbie

Musée Galliera

av. du President Wilson

George V

r. Marbeuf

av. des Champs-Elysées

W. Churchill

place de la Concorde

r. d'Iéna

Palais de Tokyo

Musée d'Art Moderne

av. de New York

quai Branly

Seine

pont de l'Alma

cours La Reine

pont de la Concorde

quai d'Orsay

pont des Invalides

pont Alexandre III

quai d'Orsay

Palais Bourbon/ Assemblée Nationale

bd. Saint-Germain

Tour Eiffel

Quai Branly

av. de la Bourdonnais

av. Elisée Reclus

av. Bosquet

r. de l'Université

Maréchal Gallieni

r. Saint-Dominique

bd. de La Tour Maubourg

r. de l'Université

INVALIDES

r. Saint-Dominique

av. Gustave Eiffel

Parc du

av. Emile Deschanel

r. Saint-Dominique

Esplanade des Invalides

Institut Géographique National

r. de Bellechasse

av. Charles Floquet

av. de Suffren

Champ de Mars

av. de la Bourdonnais

r. de Grenelle

av. de La Motte Picquet

Hôtel des Invalides

7e

r. de Varenne

av. E. Acollas

av. de la Motte Picquet

av. Duquesne

av. de Tourville

bd. des Invalides

r. Vaneau

15e

Ecole Militaire

av. de Lowendal

av. d'Estrées

place du Président Mithouard

r. de Babylone

r. Vaneau

av. de Suffren

UNESCO

av. de Saxe

av. Duquesne

av. de Saxe

bd. des Invalides

r. de Sèvres

r. du Commerce

r. Frémicourt

bd. Garibaldi

av. de Suffren

av. de Breteuil

r. de Sèvres

bd. du Montparnasse

r. du Cherche Midi

r. Lecourbe

place Henri Queuille

0 — 1/2 mi

0 — 0.5 km

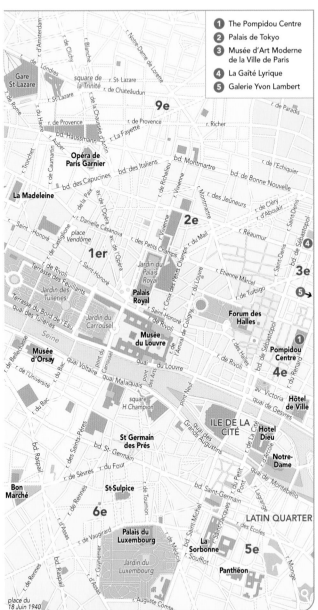

1. The Pompidou Centre
2. Palais de Tokyo
3. Musée d'Art Moderne de la Ville de Paris
4. La Gaîté Lyrique
5. Galerie Yvon Lambert

Y ou only have to look at the Louvre's glass pyramid or the Pompidou Centre's madcap building to realize that Parisians can be unconventional when they put their minds to it—something that's also reflected in the city's art scene. This tour guides you through Paris's biggest contemporary art venues, plus a selection of its interesting smaller galleries. If you're looking for something more alternative, check out www.tram-idf.fr (in French), which runs an "art bus" called Taxi Tram that ships you between Paris's hottest venues two Saturdays a month (☎ 01-53-19-73-50). START: **Métro to Rambuteau.**

The Pompidou Centre houses Europe's biggest collection of modern art.

❶ kids ★★★ The Pompidou Centre. This benchmark art venue, designed by Richard Rogers and Renzo Piano, is one of the best-known sites in Paris, holding the largest collection of modern art in Europe. The permanent collections cover 20th- and 21st-century art, with some 40,000 rotating works. The fifth floor is dedicated to modern art from 1905 to 1960 (fauvism, cubism, interwar art, surrealism, abstraction, and neorealism). Floor 4 covers 1960 to the modern day, providing themed rooms that focus on such movements as antiform art (*arte povera*) and video installations. Go it alone, or opt for the English audio-guided visit. There's a special children's guide for 6- to 12-year-olds. But whatever you do, don't miss the masterpiece on the top floor—a stunning view of Paris. ⏱ *2 hr. Place Georges Pompidou, 4th.* ☎ *01-44-78-12-33. www.centre-pompidou.fr. Admission 11€ –13€ ages 26 & over, 9€–10€ students & ages 18–25, free for children 17 & under & visitors 25 & under from E.U. countries. Wed–Mon 11am–10pm (until midnight for some exhibitions & 11pm Thurs). Métro: Rambuteau or Hôtel de Ville. RER: Châtelet-les-Halles.*

❷ ★ Palais de Tokyo. This "Site de Création Contemporaine" is a showcase for experimental art

The Palais de Tokyo is the place in Paris for contemporary art installations.

A visitor takes in a Modigliani at the Musée d'Art Moderne de la Ville de Paris.

on a big scale. Inside its stripped-back interior, selected artists (such as Pierre Joseph and Wang Du) fill the space with temporary exhibitions of whatever weird eccentricities they can muster. Visit this cutting-edge gallery if you enjoy having your perception of art challenged. ⓘ *2 hr. 13 av. du President Wilson, 16th.* ☎ *01-81-97-35-88. www.palaisdetokyo.com. Admission 10€ ages 27 & over, 8€ ages 19–26, free for children 18 & under. Tues–Sun noon–midnight. Métro: Alma-Marceau or Iéna. RER: Pont d'Alma.*

❸ ★★ **Musée d'Art Moderne de la Ville de Paris.** Take yourself on a journey through 20th-century "isms": fauvism, cubism, surrealism, realism, expressionism, and neorealism to be exact, with works by such artists as Braque, Dufy, Picasso, Léger, and Matisse, all presented in chronological order. In addition to the permanent collection, expect more fascinating retrospectives on major 20th-century artistic movements, plus thematic exhibitions on the best of today's artistic pickings. *11 av. du Président Wilson, 16th.* ☎ *01-53-67-40-00. www.mam.paris.fr. Free admission for permanent collections; temporary collections 5€–11€ adults, free for children 17 & under. Tues–Sun 10am–6pm (until 10pm Thurs for*

temporary exhibitions). Métro: Alma-Marceau or Iéna. RER: Pont d'Alma.

❹ **La Gaîté Lyrique.** Set inside a former Belle Epoque theater, this multidisciplinary arts centre is *the* place to see digital art by both recognized and up-and-coming names. Displays are consistently cutting-edge, featuring disciplines like music, graphic design, fashion, and even video games. Electronic music concerts are held in the state-of-the-art concert hall, where every square section of wall is a speaker. *3 bis rue Papin, 3rd.* ☎ *01-53-01-52-00. www.gaite-lyrique.net. Admission 7€ ages 26 & over, 5€ ages 25 & under. Tues–Sat 2–8pm, Sun 2–6pm. Métro: Réamur-Sébastopol/Arts et Métiers.*

❺ ★ **Galerie Yvon Lambert.** Gallerist Yvon Lambert's private collection was so huge that a museum was opened in Avignon (Provence) to house it. This multidisciplinary Paris space includes a gallery where art by leading international names, such as Sol LeWitt and Jenny Holzer, is hung, a brand-new video area, and an art bookshop/basement gallery where younger artists are given precious exhibition space. *108 rue Vieille du Temple, 3rd.* ☎ *01-42-71-09-33. www.yvon-lambert.com. Tues–Sat 10am–7pm.*

Outside the Musée d'Art Moderne de la Ville de Paris.

Hemingway's Paris

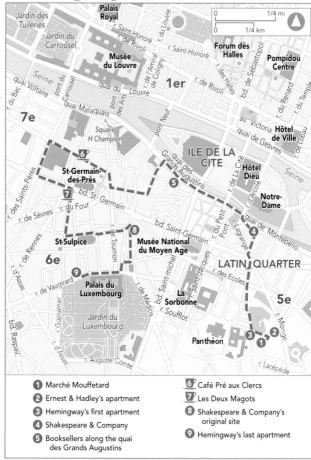

1 Marché Mouffetard
2 Ernest & Hadley's apartment
3 Hemingway's first apartment
4 Shakespeare & Company
5 Booksellers along the quai des Grands Augustins

6 Café Pré aux Clercs
7 Les Deux Magots
8 Shakespeare & Company's original site
9 Hemingway's last apartment

For fans of Papa Hemingway, a trip to Paris is a pilgrimage. This is where Hemingway honed his craft, bullied F. Scott Fitzgerald, and charmed Gertrude Stein. Here he married more than once and had countless mistresses, not the least of which was Paris herself. Oh sure, he cheated on her with Cuba and Spain, but we all know he *really* loved her. This tour follows his spectacular rise and charts the beginning of his fall. START: **Métro to Censier Daubenton.**

1 ★ Marché Mouffetard. At the beginning of his memoir, *A Moveable Feast*, Hemingway

describes spending time on Rue Mouffetard's "wonderful narrow crowded market street." That

One of the secondhand booksellers along the Quai des Grands Augustins.

description still fits—it's narrow, crowded, and wonderfully Parisian.

② Ernest & Hadley's Apartment. Several blocks up Rue Mouffetard, Rue du Cardinal-Lemoine branches off to the right. A few houses down, on the fourth floor of no. 74, a 22-year-old Hemingway and his wife Hadley rented their first Parisian apartment together. This was not Hem's first home in Paris, though—that was around the corner, on Rue Descartes. (See the next stop.) *74 rue du Cardinal-Lemoine, 5th.*

③ Hemingway's First Apartment. When he first moved to Paris as a writer for the *Toronto Star*

newspaper, Hemingway took a grimy, cheap room on the top floor of a hotel on Rue Descartes. The small wall plaque wrongly states that he lived here for 4 years—he was actually here for 1. *39 rue Descartes, 5th.*

④ ★ Shakespeare & Company. Walk toward the river for about 15 minutes, first on Rue Descartes (which joins Rue Montagne St-Geneviève) through Place Maubert, then down Rue F. Sauton, and then take a sharp left onto Rue de la Bucherie to reach Paris's best expat bookstore. In the 1920s, it was at 11 rue de l'Odéon, and it was at that location that Hemingway broke a vase when he read a bad review, that Henry Miller used to "borrow" books and never bring them back, and that James Joyce's *Ulysses* was first published. The current location is still a favorite of writers for its eccentric attitude and wonderful selection of books. ⏱ *30 min.–1 hr. 37 rue de la Bucherie, 5th.* ☎ *01-43-25-40-93. www.shakespeareandcompany.com. Mon–Fri 10am–11pm, Sat–Sun 11am–11pm. Métro: St-Michel.*

⑤ Booksellers along Quai des Grands Augustins. Hemingway frequently shopped here among the

The 1920s—Americans in Paris

The so-called Lost Generation, led by American expatriates Gertrude Stein and Alice B. Toklas, topped the list of celebrities who "occupied" Paris after World War I. Paris attracted the *littérateur, bon viveur,* and drifter, including writers Henry Miller, Ernest Hemingway, and F. Scott Fitzgerald and composer Cole Porter.

With the collapse of Wall Street, many Americans returned home. But not hard-core bohemians like Miller, who wandered around smoking Gauloises when not writing *Tropic of Cancer*. But even such die-hards as Miller eventually realized that 1930s Paris was collapsing as war clouds loomed; he left in 1939. Gertrude and Alice remained in France and are buried together (Stein died in 1946, Toklas in 1967) in the Cimetière du Père-Lachaise (p 95, ⑬).

secondhand book peddlers (called *bouquinistes*) along the edge of the Seine. Now, as then, their collections are bewilderingly eclectic—like a flea market for books. I once saw the complete Harry Potter collection, in English, next to a book of French erotica. ⏱ *30 min.–1 hr. Quai des Grands Augustins, 6th.*

6 Café Pré aux Clercs. Next you'll come to a series of cafes where you can take a well-deserved rest, as Hem surely would, over a whiskey or a glass of the house red. The first cafe is this charming one reached by walking down Rue des Grands Augustins. (No. 7 was once Pablo Picasso's studio.) Turn onto Rue St-André des Arts, and then right along Rue de Seine and left onto the antiques-shop-lined Rue Jacob, which brings you to Rue Bonaparte and this cafe. It was one of Hem's early haunts, a short walk from the Hotel d'Angleterre, where he slept (in room no.14) on his first night in Paris. *30 rue Bonaparte, 6th.* ☎ *01-83-76-16-53. www.restaurant-lepreauxclercs.com. $$–$$$.*

7 ★★ Les Deux Magots. Loop down noisy Rue des Saints-Pères to the more sophisticated hustle of Boulevard Saint-Germain, and soon you'll see the glass front of this cafe, which has gotten more mileage out of the gay '20s than any flapper ever could have. This was the preeminent hangout of the arty expat crowd, where Hemingway charmed the girls, picked fights with the critics, and hassled tourists. The feel today is admittedly touristy, and the food okay (but pricey), but it's still a good place to have a coffee and wonder what he'd think of it all now. *6 place St-Germain-des-Prés, 6th.* ☎ *01-45-48-55-25. www.lesdeuxmagots.fr. $$–$$$.*

8 **Shakespeare & Company's Original Site.** You can get in a bit of shopping at the many posh boutiques and little jewelry stores on Rue Saint-Sulpice before turning right onto Rue de l'Odéon and passing a plaque marking the site of the original Shakespeare & Company bookstore. *11 rue de l'Odéon, 6th.*

9 **Hemingway's Last Apartment.** After turning down Rue de Vaugirard and walking past the French Senate, look for this narrow lane near the Jardins du Luxembourg. The impressive building at no. 6 was Hemingway's last Paris apartment. My, how the fallen became mighty. From the look of its medallions, sphinxes, and heavy gates, you might get the idea that he'd written a successful novel *(The Sun Also Rises)* and left poor Hadley for somebody richer (Pauline Pfeiffer). And so he had. Here, he reached the summit of his success, and his descent into alcoholism began. *6 rue Férou, 6th.* ●

Un serveur *at Les Deux Magots in Saint-Germain-des-Prés.*

MICKAEL MARCIANO

The Latin Quarter

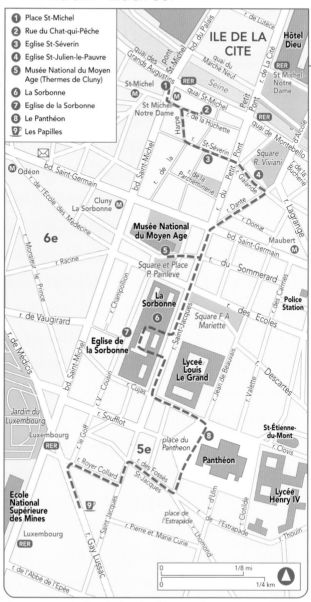

1 Place St-Michel
2 Rue du Chat-qui-Pêche
3 Eglise St-Séverin
4 Eglise St-Julien-le-Pauvre
5 Musée National du Moyen Age (Thermes de Cluny)
6 La Sorbonne
7 Eglise de la Sorbonne
8 Le Panthéon
9 Les Papilles

Previous page: Under the vaulted arcades of the Marais district.

In the 1920s, this Left Bank neighborhood was the heart of Parisian cafe society. You'll still find plenty of cafes, plus universities and shops, all constantly buzzing with activity. Traditionally arty, intellectual, and bohemian, the area also has a history of political unrest. Today, it is still one of Paris's most interesting, not to mention picturesque, quarters to explore. **Start: Métro to St-Michel.**

1 Place Saint-Michel. An elaborate 1860 fountain of Saint Michael presides over this bustling cafe- and shop-lined square, where skirmishes between occupying Germans and French Resistance fighters once took place. This is the beginning of busy Boulevard Saint-Michel, which was trendy long ago but is now a disappointing line of fast-food chains and down-market stores. It is, however, the main student quarters, and a young, lively atmosphere pervades.

2 Rue du Chat-qui-Pêche. Turn left down Rue de la Huchette, bypassing its endless kabob and pizza joints to reach this street, which is one of the narrowest in Paris, at just 1.80m (6 ft.) wide. Plenty of local tales exist about the history of the name ("Street of the Cat Who Fishes"), but nobody knows for sure.

3 Eglise Saint-Séverin. This charming medieval church was built in the early 13th century and reconstructed in the 15th. Don't miss the gargoyles and monsters projecting from the roof. Inside, linger over the rare Georges Rouault etchings from the 1920s. ⏱ *30 min. 1 rue des Pretres St-Séverin, 5th.* ☎ *01-42-34-93-50. www.saint-severin.com. Mon–Sat 11am–7:30pm, Sun 9am–8:30pm.*

4 Eglise Saint-Julien-le-Pauvre. Take Rue Saint-Séverin to Rue Galande and, after snapping photos of its quaint old houses, find this medieval church, which dates, at least in part, to 1170. Note the unusual capitals covered in carved vines and leaves. The garden contains one of the oldest trees in Paris and has one of my favorite views of Notre-Dame. ⏱ *20 min. Rue St-Julien-le-Pauvre, 5th.* ☎ *01-43-54-52-16. http://sjlpmelkites.fr. Mon–Sat 9:30am–noon & 3–6:30pm. Métro: Cluny–La Sorbonne.*

5 ★★ Musée National du Moyen Age–Thermes de

The Fontaine Saint-Michel, at the center of Place Saint-Michel.

The Lady and the Unicorn tapestries at the Musée National du Moyen Age.

Cluny. With one of the world's strongest collections of medieval art, this small, manageable museum is a gem. Most visitors come to see the *Lady and the Unicorn* tapestries, but there's much more here than long-haired maidens and mythical creatures: This 15th-century Gothic building sits atop 2nd-century baths. The Gallo-Roman pools are in excellent shape—the frigidarium (cold bath) and tepidarium (warm bath) can still be clearly seen (although you can no longer take a dip). ⏱ *1 hr. 6 place Paul-Painlevé, 5th.* ☎ *01-53-73-78-00. www.musee-moyenage.fr. Admission* *8€ ages 26 & over, 6€ ages 18–26 from outside E.U., free for ages 25 & under from E.U. countries & 17 & under from outside E.U.; free for everyone 1st Sun of the month. Wed–Mon 9:15am–5:45pm. Métro: Cluny–La Sorbonne.*

⑥ ★ La Sorbonne. France's most famous university, dating back some 700 years, has all the venerable buildings and confident, scraggly-haired students you might imagine. Teachers here have included Thomas Aquinas, and the alumni association counts Dante, Calvin, and Longfellow among its past members. This is a sprawling

A bulwark of higher education in the French capital: La Sorbonne.

Le Panthéon, an 18th-century memorial hall honoring France's greatest intellectuals.

place, and only the courtyard and galleries are open to the public (9am–5pm) when school is in session—follow the crowds and the scarce signs to get a peek. Or book a guided tour (in French only; Mon–Fri and one Sat per month). ⏱ *30 min. 12 rue de la Sorbonne, 5th.* ☎ *01-40-46-22-11. www. sorbonne.fr. Admission for guided tour 9€. Métro: Cluny–La Sorbonne.*

❼ ★ Eglise de la Sorbonne. On the grounds of the Sorbonne, this 17th-century church holds the elaborate tomb of Cardinal Richelieu (1585–1642). Richelieu was a staunch defender of the monarchy's power and did much to unify the French state. The extraordinary statue at its feet is poignantly named *Learning in Tears;* the figure mourning at the cardinal's feet represents science, and the one supporting him represents religion. ⏱ *30 min. Rue de la Sorbonne, 5th.*

❽ ★★ Le Panthéon. This magnificent building was built by Louis XV as a tribute to Saint Geneviève. (Construction began in 1758.) Since the Revolution, however, it's been used to honor more earthly heroes. France's great dead are entombed here, including Voltaire, Rousseau, Zola, and Hugo. Recent additions

include Marie Curie, whose remains were moved here in 1995, and Alexandre Dumas, who arrived in 2002. Appropriately, Foucault's pendulum is here—the famous device, which proved that the Earth rotates on an axis, was said to hang from "the eye of God." Although the pendulum appears to swing, it's not moving—the Earth is. ⏱ *1 hr. Place du Panthéon, 5th.* ☎ *01-44-32-18-00;http://pantheon.monuments-nationaux.fr. Admission 7.50€ ages 26 & over, 4.50€ ages 18–26 from outside E.U., free for ages 25 & under from E.U. countries & 17 & under from outside E.U. Daily 10am–6pm (Apr–Sept until 6:30pm). Métro: Cardinal Lemoine. RER: Luxembourg.*

❾ Les Papilles. Dying for a break? This is just the place. The owners of this sweet Provençal-style cafe are dedicated to Southern French food and adventurous wine. The small menu changes with the seasons, and the wines change with the owners' moods. If it's available, try the excellent stewed chicken or the hearty cassoulet. *30 rue Gay-Lussac, 5th.* ☎ *01-43-25-20-79. www.lespapillesparis.fr. RER: Luxembourg. $$.*

Saint-Germain-des-Prés

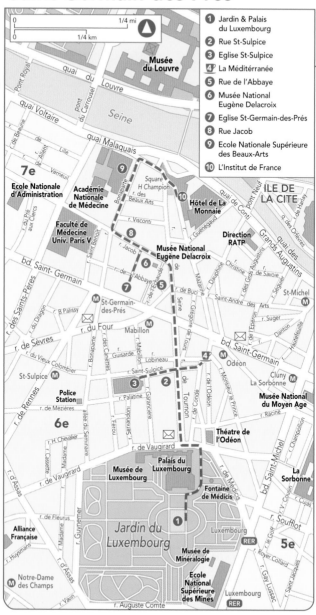

1. Jardin & Palais du Luxembourg
2. Rue St-Sulpice
3. Eglise St-Sulpice
4. La Méditérranée
5. Rue de l'Abbaye
6. Musée National Eugène Delacroix
7. Eglise St-Germain-des-Prés
8. Rue Jacob
9. Ecole Nationale Supérieure des Beaux-Arts
10. L'Institut de France

This neighborhood was the place to be in the 1920s. Here the literati met the glitterati and *tout* Paris marveled at the ensuing explosion of creativity and alcoholism. On these streets, Sartre fumed, while Hemingway and Fitzgerald drank and quarreled. Today the bookshops have been replaced by designer boutiques, but it's still the place to go for a night on the town. START: **Métro to Luxembourg.**

❶ ★★★ kids Jardins & Palais du Luxembourg. There's a certain justice in the fact that this former palace, built between 1615 and 1627 for the widow of Henry IV, is now home to the democratically elected French Senate. The lovely Italianate building also houses the Musée du Luxembourg, famed for its world-class temporary art exhibitions (19 rue de Vaugirard, 6th; ☎ 01-40-13-62-00; www.museedu luxembourg.fr). Most people, however, come for the gardens. The picturesque paths of the Jardins du Luxembourg have always been a favorite of artists, although children, students from the nearby Sorbonne, and tourists are more common than painters nowadays. Hemingway claimed to have survived a winter by catching pigeons here for his supper, and Gertrude Stein used to cross the gardens on her way to sit for Picasso. The classic formal gardens are well-groomed and symmetrically designed. And there are statues everywhere—more than 80

of them vie for your attention—a long-haired French queen, a nymph playing a flute, a stern effigy of poet Charles Baudelaire. It's fanciful and delightful; you could spend hours here and not discover all its secrets. Particularly popular with families are the pond in which children float wooden boats, the games area, and pétanque (French boules) pitches. ⏲ *1 hr. Métro: Odéon. RER: Luxembourg.*

❷ Place & Rue Saint-Sulpice. Turn down any street on the river side of the gardens and walk a few blocks to Place Saint-Sulpice and its surrounding streets. Welcome to shopping heaven (or window-shopping purgatory). This is where you'll find all the usual designer suspects for your inspection—agnès b., YSL, perfumer Annick Goutal, and more. If you want to stock up for a picnic, pop down to 8 rue du Cherche-Midi to Poilâne bakery for some of the city's best breads and sandwiches to go. Or turn onto Rue Bonaparte,

Like Les Deux Magots across the street, Café Flore has been a neighborhood institution for decades.

A merry-go-round in the Luxembourg Gardens.

where Pierre Hermé (at no. 72) makes the city's most delicious macaroons (p 105).

③ ★★ Eglise Saint-Sulpice.

Filled with paintings by Delacroix, including *Jacob's Fight with the Angel*, this is a wonderful church in which to meditate and take in some gorgeous frescoes. The church has one of the world's largest organs, comprising 6,700 pipes—a national treasure, especially when it's played. ⏱ *30 min. Rue St-Sulpice, 6th.* ☎ *01-42-34-59-98. http://pss75.fr/saint-sulpice-paris/. Daily 7:30am–7:30pm.*

④ La Méditérranée.

A short walk away lies this restaurant, filled with murals by 20th-century stage designers Christian Bérard and Marcel Vertés and paintings by Picasso and Chagall. It was once a haunt of Jacqueline Kennedy, Picasso, and Jean Cocteau (whose work enlivens the plates and menus). The chef delivers creative interpretations of traditional dishes, including delicious fried fish with fresh spinach salad, and an incredible bouillabaisse, thick with seafood. The prix-fixe menu ranges from 28€ to 35€. *2 place de l'Odéon, 6th.* ☎ *01-43-26-02-30. www.la-mediterranee.com. Métro: Odéon. $$$.*

⑤ Rue de l'Abbaye.

Saint-Germain was built around an old abbey that once towered over this street, although there's virtually nothing left of it today. With houses and churches built from brick, the street is charming, particularly Rue de Furstenberg—once the abbot's stables, it's now filled with upscale interior design shops.

⑥ ★ Musée National Eugène Delacroix.

The Romantic painter Eugène Delacroix lived and worked in this lovely house on Rue de Furstenberg from 1857 until his death in 1863. The museum sits on a charming square and has a romantic garden. Most of his major works are in the Louvre, but the collection here is unusually personal, including an early self-portrait and letters and notes to such friends as Baudelaire and George Sand. You can also see his work in the Chapelle

The mighty pipe organ at Eglise Saint-Sulpice.

des Anges in Eglise Saint-Sulpice (see ❸ on this tour). ⏱ *1 hr. 6 rue de Furstenberg, 6th.* ☎ *01-44-41-86-50. www.musee-delacroix.fr. Admission 5€ adults, free for children 17 & under & visitors 25 & under from E.U. countries. Wed–Mon 9:30am–5pm. Métro: St-Germain-des-Prés.*

❼ ★ **Eglise Saint-Germain-des-Prés.** This exquisite little church is the oldest in Paris, and a rarity in France—only a few buildings this old exist in such complete form. It dates to the 6th century, when a Benedictine abbey was founded here, although little remains from that time. Its aged columns still bear their medieval paint in breathtaking detail. You can visit the tomb of the French philosopher René Descartes (1596–1650) in the second chapel. At one time, the abbey was a pantheon for Merovingian kings. During the restoration of their tombs, Chapelle de Saint-Symphorien, previously unknown Romanesque paintings were discovered. ⏱ *30 min. 3 place St-Germain-des-Prés, 6th.* ☎ *01-55-42-81-10. www.eglise-sgp.org. Mon–Sat 8am–7:45pm, Sun 9am–8pm. Métro: St-Germain-des-Prés.*

❽ **Rue Jacob.** This elegant street, with clean lines and classic 19th-century architecture, was once home to such illustrious residents as the author Colette and the composer Richard Wagner. Today, it holds charming bookstores and antiques shops and is all very posh-bohemian.

❾ **Ecole Nationale Supérieure des Beaux-Arts.** Turn onto Rue Bonaparte and walk toward the river to reach this fine-arts school, where the main attraction is the architecture. The school occupies a 17th-century convent and the 18th-century Hôtel de Chimay. Attending an exhibition (held frequently) will grant you a peek inside, but if none is on, just wander down Rue

Bonaparte, which is lined with lovely small art galleries. ⏱ *30 min. 14 rue Bonaparte, 6th.* ☎ *01-47-03-50-00. www.ensba.fr. Courtyard Mon–Fri 9am–5pm; during exhibitions Tues–Sun 1–7pm. Métro: St-Germain-des-Prés.*

❿ **L'Institut de France.** Turn right along the river and you'll see a hard-to-miss elegant domed baroque building, home to five subgovernmental agencies all lumped together as the rather ominously named L'Institut. Here the Académie Française zealously (some would say too zealously) guards the purity of the French language from "Franglais" encroachment (Jacques Cousteau was once a member), while other, lesser-known agencies (Sciences, Inscriptions et Belles Lettres, Beaux Arts, and Sciences Morales et Politiques) do . . . whatever it is they do. The brave can arrange for a guided tour (available in English) as all buildings are closed to the public—perhaps not surprisingly, considering that academy members are known as "the Immortals." ⏱ *15 min. 23 quai de Conti, 6th.* ☎ *01-44-41-44-41. www.institut-de-france.fr. Guided tours 2nd Sun of the month (request via website only). Métro: St-Germain-des-Prés.*

A painting at the Musée National Eugène Delacroix.

The Islands

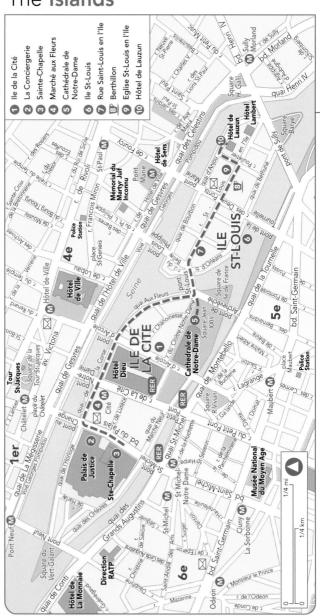

The Île de la Cité is where it all began. By the time the Romans came in 52 B.C., the Celtic Parisii tribe had been living on the Île de la Cité for about 200 years. Over the next 2 millennia, Paris was expanded by the Romans, Franks, Merovingians, and Capetian kings, but the city's soul remains here, around Notre-Dame cathedral. Across the pont Saint-Louis, Île Saint-Louis (former marshlands) is a coveted residential area filled with glorious 17th-century mansions. This tour takes you through both islands and along some of the loveliest stretches of the Seine. START: **Métro to Cité.**

❶ Île de la Cité. By medieval times, this was a thriving island town with huddles of houses and narrow streets. But it was all swept away in the 19th century by Baron Haussmann when he evicted some 25,000 people to make way for the large administrative buildings we see today, such as the law courts and police station. Few have written more movingly about its heyday than Victor Hugo, who invites the reader "to observe the fantastic display of lights against the darkness of that gloomy labyrinth of buildings; cast upon it a ray of moonlight, showing the city in glimmering vagueness, with its towers lifting their great heads from that foggy sea." You have only to climb Notre-Dame's towers to see what he's talking about: On a cloudy day, the skies look dramatic and cast eerie light over the island. Linking the Île de la Cité to the city at large is the pont Neuf, embellished by a statue of Henri IV. The name means "new bridge"—ironic considering that it's Paris's oldest bridge, dating back to the 16th century.

❷ ★ La Conciergerie. This intimidating building, originally a medieval royal palace, was converted into a prison during the Revolution and became an object of terror at a time when idle accusations could result in spontaneous

Pont des Arts, near the islands, was built in the 1980s as a copy of an original 19th-century bridge.

La Conciergerie, with a view toward the pont Neuf.

executions. Marie Antoinette, Danton, and Robespierre all were held here before being guillotined. Today, you can see the cells where they were held and the rooms where they were tried and condemned. A strange and interesting place. *See p 23,* ③.

③ ★ **Sainte-Chapelle.** Tucked away among the huge Conciergerie and the vast law courts of the Palais de Justice, this tiny church is as hard to find as a diamond in a coal mine—but persevere, because it's a precious place, made almost entirely of dazzling stained-glass windows. Unfortunately, it's not undiscovered, and I've found it in the past by following the crowds to a long line waiting to get in. *See p 23,* ③.

④ **Marché aux Fleurs.** This vivid flower market is a photo opportunity simply crying out for your camera. It must be one of the most photographed places in the city— and for good reason. On Sunday, it's transformed into a bird market, but the standard of living for the animals presented is questionable. ⏱ *30 min. Place Louis Lépine, Quai*

de la Corse, Quai des Fleurs, 4th. Mon–Sat 8am–7:30pm, Sun 8am–7pm. Métro: Cité.

⑤ ★★★ **Cathédrale Notre-Dame.** This world-famous cathedral is more beautiful in person than on film. Climb its towers to see malicious gargoyles and sweeping panoramas of the city. *See p 9,* ⑦.

⑥ **Île Saint-Louis.** Despite its central location, the Île Saint-Louis still feels like a tranquil backwater, removed, somehow, from the rest of the buzzing city. The 17th-century buildings lining the narrow streets are some of the city's most expensive properties, and many of them have hosted, at one point or another, French literary stars, such as Racine and Molière. A bourgeois arty crowd still frequents the many art galleries around. It's a lovely place to wander and so tiny that it's almost impossible to get lost.

⑦ **Rue Saint-Louis-en-l'Île.** The Île Saint-Louis's central artery is gorgeous, narrow, and lined with restaurants and boutiques selling art, clothes, precious stones and minerals, food, hats, and jewelry. Hôtel Chenizot, at no. 51, has fantastic carved dragons and bearded fauns on its facade. If you can, go through the door and admire the sculpted facade in the courtyard beyond. A second courtyard also contains craft shops and galleries. The end of the street closest to the Île de la Cité is a great place to get a photo of Notre-Dame.

8 Berthillon. On Île Saint-Louis, even the ice-cream stores are sophisticated. This place proves it, with polite crowds queuing outside for cones to go, and others perched at the tables inside to try the lemon, hazelnut, and mango flavors favored by the locals—the chocolate is especially divine. *31 rue St-Louis-en-l'Île, 4th. Métro: Pont Marie. $.*

9 Eglise Saint-Louis-en-l'Île. This 17th-century church, vastly overshadowed by Notre-Dame , has wonderful rococo-baroque architecture, including a lovely sunburst above the altar. Not as dramatic as its famous neighbor, but it's more intimate and enchanting. ⏱ *20 min. 19 rue St-Louis-en-l'Île, 4th.* ☎ *01-46-34-11-60. www.saint-louisenlile.catholique.fr Tues–Sun 9am–noon & 3–7pm. Métro: Pont Marie.*

10 ★★ Hôtel Lauzun. This astonishing place, with fantastic drains in the shapes of sea serpents, was the scene of famously long, hazy hashish parties thrown by poets Baudelaire and Théophile Gautier. Baudelaire wrote *Les Fleurs du Mal* while living here, although it's hard to see how he could have been so depressed living somewhere so pretty. The building takes its name from a former occupant, the duc de Lauzun. He was a favorite of Louis XIV until he asked for the hand of the king's cousin, the duchesse de Montpensier. Louis refused and had Lauzun tossed into the Bastille. Eventually, the duchesse convinced Louis to release him, and they married secretly and moved here in 1682. *17 quai d'Anjou. Generally closed to the public, although sometimes there are art exhibits here—check with the tourist office. Métro: Pont Marie.*

It's worth the wait for a glimpse inside Sainte-Chapelle, made almost entirely of stained glass.

The **Marais**

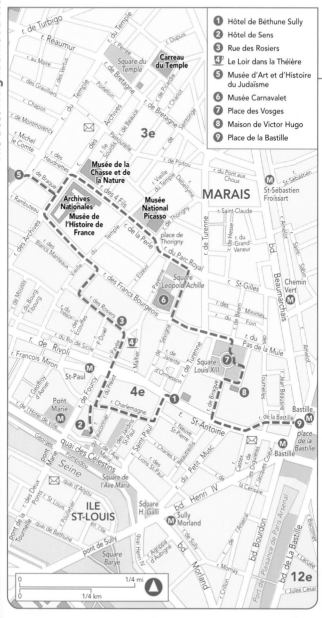

1 Hôtel de Béthune Sully
2 Hôtel de Sens
3 Rue des Rosiers
4 Le Loir dans la Théière
5 Musée d'Art et d'Histoire du Judaïsme
6 Musée Carnavalet
7 Place des Vosges
8 Maison de Victor Hugo
9 Place de la Bastille

When the Île de la Cité became overcrowded in the 17th century, it was here, to what had been swampland, that the wealthy Parisians moved, filling the streets with fashionable mansions called *hôtels*. Over the years, it became the center of the city's Jewish community, although today the gay and lesbian community has adopted the area. Its many boutiques and diverse buildings make for excellent shopping and exploring. START: **Métro to St-Paul.**

1 Hôtel de Béthune-Sully. Out of the Métro, turn right on Rue Saint-Antoine and walk through the wooden doorway at no. 62. The relief-studded facade of this gracious mansion dazzles just as much as when it was first designed as the residence of the family of Maximilien de Béthune, duke of Sully, Henri IV's famous minister, in 1625. It stands as one of the finest Louis XIII structures in Paris and, although the building is closed to the public, a bookshop and the charming walled garden are open during office hours (and on weekends from around 9am–6pm). A "secret" door leads to the Place des Vosges (see **7**, below). ⏱ *30 min. 62 rue St-Antoine, 4th. http://sully.monuments-nationaux.fr. Métro: St-Paul.*

The Hôtel de Sens once housed the arch-bishops of Sens.

The Hôtel de Béthune-Sully is one of the finest 17th-century buildings in Paris.

2 Hôtel de Sens. Given the leaded windows and fairy-tale turrets, you might not be surprised to find that this 15th-century mansion has a gloriously ornate courtyard in which you can wander at will most afternoons. Once a private home for archbishops and, later, queens, it now holds a fine-arts library, the Bibliothèque Forney. ⏱ *20 min. 1 rue du Figuier.* ☎ *01-42-78-14-60. Courtyard Tues & Fri–Sat 1:30–7:30pm, Wed–Thurs 10am–7:30pm. Métro: St-Paul.*

3 Rue des Rosiers. Perhaps the most colorful and typical street remaining from the time when this was the city's Jewish quarter, Rue des Rosiers (Street of the Rose-bushes) meanders among the old buildings with nary a rose to be seen. It is jam-packed with falafel cafes and shops, though, and makes a plum spot for a cheap lunch.

4 ★ **Le Loir dans la Théière.** This bustling cafe serves some of the best homemade cakes in the Marais. There's usually a queue to get a table, but it's worth the wait—if only for the humongous lemon meringue pies (7€ a slice). The quiches and salads are good too (from 12€). *3 rue des Rosiers, 4th.* ☎ *01-42-72-90-61. $.*

5 ★ **Musée d'Art et d'Histoire du Judaïsme.** This museum was created in 1948 to protect the city's Jewish history after the Holocaust. It's a moving place, with excellent Jewish decorative arts from around Europe—German Hanukkah lamps, a wooden sukkah cabin from Austria—and documents related to the continent's Jewish history. There's also a memorial to the Jews who lived in the building in 1939, 13 of whom died in concentration camps. ⏱ *45 min. Hôtel de St-Aignan, 71 rue du Temple, 3rd.* ☎ *01-53-01-86-60. www.mahj.org. Mon–Fri 11am–6pm, Sun 10am–6pm. Admission*

6.80€ ages 27 & up, free for ages 26 & under. Métro: Rambuteau.

6 **Musée Carnavalet.** The Renaissance palace that houses this free museum was acquired by Mme de Carnavalet (hence its name), but is most associated with the letter-writing Mme de Sévigné, who moved here in 1677 to be with her daughter and poured out nearly every detail of her life in her letters, virtually ignoring her son. Several salons cover the Revolution, and others display furniture from the Louis XIV period to the early 20th century, including a replica of Marcel Proust's cork-lined bedroom. Also on view are the chessmen Louis XVI used to distract himself while waiting to go to the guillotine. ⏱ *1 hr. 23 rue de Sévigné, 3rd.* ☎ *01-44-59-58-58. www.carnavalet. paris.fr. Tues–Sun 10am–6pm. Free admission. Métro: St-Paul or Chemin Vert.*

7 **Place des Vosges.** This is Paris's oldest square and was once its most fashionable; today it's arguably its most adorable, with

A cafe on the colorful Rue des Rosiers.

The meticulously manicured topiary of the Musée Carnavalet.

perfect brick-and-stone pavilions rising above covered arcades. Its perfect symmetry might be why so many writers and artists (Descartes, Pascal, Gautier, and Hugo) chose to live here. *See p 14,* ⑤.

⑧ Maison de Victor Hugo.

The writer of *Les Misérables* lived here from 1832 to 1848, and his home has been turned into a small shrine, with period rooms dedicated to his life and works. Room 3 is particularly impressive as an Oriental-style medley of black, green, and red panels and porcelain based on the Chinese room at Hauteville Fairy in Guernsey, where Hugo's mistress, Juliette Drouet, lived during the couple's exile from France (after Napoleon III's coup d'état). It won't take you more than half an hour to go around the rooms, but there are some interesting pieces, such as his inkwell and some of his furniture. The views from the windows also offer an interesting panorama over the pink-brick Place des Vosges. ⏱ *30 min. 6 place des Vosges, 4th.* ☎ *01-42-72-10-16. Free admission. Tues–Sun 10am–6pm. Métro: St-Paul or Bastille.*

⑨ ★ **Place de la Bastille.** Nothing but a few stones on Métro line 5 at Bastille station remain of the towered fortress that once stood here (and held such prisoners as the "Man in the Iron Mask" and the Marquis de Sade). But it's worth a stop to commemorate the place where the Revolution began on July 14, 1789. *See p 14,* ⑦.

Life was far from miserable for Victor Hugo when he lived in the rooms of what is now the Maison de Victor Hugo.

Montmartre & the Sacré Coeur

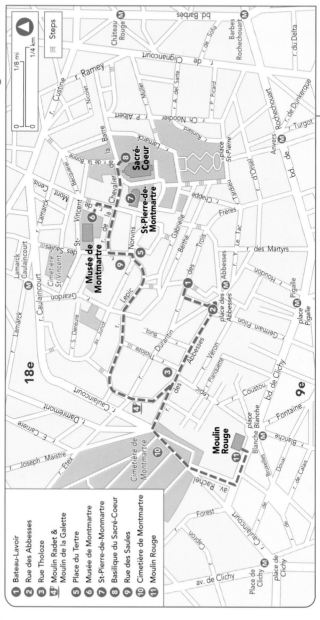

1 Bateau-Lavoir
2 Rue des Abbesses
3 Rue Tholoze
4 Moulin Radet &
   Moulin de la Galette
5 Place du Tertre
6 Musée de Montmartre
7 St-Pierre-de-Monmartre
8 Basilique du Sacré-Coeur
9 Rue des Saules
10 Cimetière de Montmartre
11 Moulin Rouge

Artsy, graceful, undulating Montmartre does something to your heart. From the moment you see its narrow, tilting houses, still windmills, and steep streets, you're in love. This part of town—known as the La Butte, or "the Hill" in the 18th arrondissement—was a rural village separate from Paris until 1860. Then, in the 1880s, Renoir and Toulouse-Lautrec helped make it a lair of artists—a legacy that lives on today. It all starts at the Abbesses Métro station—designed by French architect Hector Guimard, it's one of only two stations in Paris to still have its original Art Nouveau roof (the other is Porte Dauphine, in the 16th). START: **Métro to Abbesses.**

Views are sweeping from the steep streets and open-air staircases of Montmartre.

1 Bateau-Lavoir. This building is called the "cradle of cubism." While living here from 1904 to 1912, Picasso painted *The Third Rose* (of Gertrude Stein) and *Les Demoiselles d'Avignon*. Today, it's filled with art studios, with some occasionally open to view. ⏱ *10 min. 13 place Emile Goudeau. Métro: Abbesses.*

2 Rue des Abbesses. On this street, the unusual rust-red church with the turquoise mosaics is the neo-Gothic Saint-Jean-de-Montmartre, built early in the 20th century. Peek inside to see its delicately weaving arches. Many excellent cafes and dress shops line this street.

3 Rue Tholoze. Rue des Abbesses soon brings you to this steep, narrow street, with an adorable windmill at the top. Halfway up is Studio 28, which was the city's first proper art-house cinema, named after the year it opened. It showed Buñuel's *L'Age d'Or* in 1930, and outraged locals ripped the screen from the wall. Today, it still shows arty flicks and has a tiny bar.

4 Moulin Radet & Moulin de la Galette. The Moulin Radet windmill, confusingly enough, tops a restaurant called Le Moulin de la Galette, after the dance hall that once stood here, inspiring such artists as Renoir. The food here is traditionally French and moderately priced. *83 rue Lepic.* ☎ *01-46-06-84-77. www.lemoulindela galette.fr. $$.*

5 Place du Tertre. This old square would be lovely were it not for the tourists—and the artists chasing you around, threatening to draw your caricature. You can buy some very good original paintings here, but you'll have to haggle to

The neighborhood's history comes to life at the Musée de Montmartre.

get a reasonable price. The perpetual hubbub can be entertaining—it's charming and awful all at once.

6 Musée de Montmartre. This isn't exactly a must-see, but if you're genuinely curious about the history of this neighborhood, it is an oasis of calm and will give you a

This moulin (windmill), atop Rue Tholoze, is the subject of a recently authenticated van Gogh painting.

good look at its past. There are pictures of 19th-century Montmartre, rural and lined with windmills, along with a few Toulouse-Lautrec posters and the like. ⓘ *20 min. 12 rue Cortot, 8th.* ☎ *01-49-25-89-37. www.museedemontmartre.fr. Admission 9€ ages 27 & over, 7€ ages 12–26, free for children 11 & under. Daily 10am–6pm. Métro: Abbesses.*

7 Saint-Pierre-de-Montmartre. Follow the winding roads ever upward to this early-Gothic Benedictine abbey, now a small church. This is one of the city's oldest churches (from 1133), and its simplicity in the shadow of the Sacré Coeur is refreshing. ⓘ *15 min. Rue du Mont-Cenis.*

8 ★★ Sacré Coeur. The creamy white domes of this basilica soar high above Paris. Inside is an artistic and architectural explosion of color and form; out front are sweeping views of the gorgeous city in soft pastels. Unmissable. *See p 17, 2.*

9 Rue des Saules. Head down Rue des Saules, pausing to admire the oft-photographed nightclub Au

Lapin Agile, which was a favorite hangout of Picasso's back when it was called Cabaret des Assassins. It's still usually crowded with tourists, strange fans of old French music, and those seeking Picasso's muse. Opposite, notice the small patch of vines, a throwback from the days when Montmartre was a wine-growing village separate from Paris. The Clos Montmartre harvest (red wine) is celebrated annually in October over a very boozy weekend.

⑩ ★★ Cimetière de Montmartre.

Retrace your steps and follow Rue Lepic back down past no. 54, where van Gogh lived with his brother Theo. Turn right onto Rue Joseph-de-Maistre and then left onto Rue Caulaincourt to this quiet resting place. Get a map from the gatehouse (there's a stack on the desk)—it will help you find the graves of Truffaut, Stendhal, Degas, and many others. But don't follow it too closely—it doesn't list most of the graceful statues of exquisitely tragic women draped across tombs, nor does it tell you where the most beautiful trees stand, or where the light dapples through just so. You'll have to discover those treasures on your own. ① *1 hr. Access on Rue Rachel by stairs from Rue Caulaincourt, 18th.* ☎ *01-53-42-36-30. Free admission. Mon–Sat 8am–6pm, Sun 9am–6pm (Mar 16–Nov 5 until 5:30pm). Métro: Blanche.*

⑪ Moulin Rouge.

Immortalized by Toulouse-Lautrec (and more recently, Nicole Kidman), this bright red windmill hasn't changed much with time. Just as the windmill remains outside, the cancan still goes on inside. It's all just as tawdry and tacky as it was when Toulouse-Lautrec downed one absinthe after another to endure it, but it's the only place in Paris that still performs the real cancan. *See p 131.*

Iconic Sacré Coeur crowns the highest summit in Paris.

Canal Saint-Martin & Villette

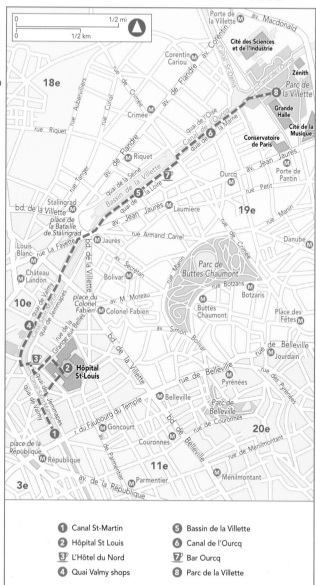

1 Canal St-Martin
2 Hôpital St Louis
3 L'Hôtel du Nord
4 Quai Valmy shops

5 Bassin de la Villette
6 Canal de l'Ourcq
7 Bar Ourcq
8 Parc de la Villette

This tour will take you past legacies of early-20th-century industrialized Paris—its tree-lined piers, iron footbridges, old factories, and warehouses—relics that evoke the days when Edith Piaf lifted the spirits of the nation with her soulful "La Vie en Rose" (1946). Today, this area, both scruffy and cosmopolitan, is the most happening district in the city. Its bohemian vibe and new canal-side galleries, cafes, and shops make it a fun place to stroll. In summer, the Parc de la Villette—with its science and music museums, IMAX cinema, and open-air film festival—is a hip place to see and be seen. START: **Métro to République.**

1 ★ **Canal Saint-Martin.** Walk across Place de la République to Rue Beaurepaire, lined with trendy shops and cafes. At the end of the street, you're on Quai de Valmy. The Canal Saint-Martin, built between 1805 and 1825, begins at Bastille but hides underground until Boulevard Richard Lenoir nearby. This is the prettiest stretch, lined with chestnut trees and iron footbridges that beg to be photographed. If you saw the film *Amélie*, it was here she skimmed stones.

Opposite Rue Beaurepaire, cross the footbridge and go up Avenue Richerand.

2 **Hôpital Saint-Louis.** The Saint-Louis hospital was founded by Henri IV to house plague victims away from the city center and was built in the same style as Place des Vosges (p 14). Enter and then leave via the left wing, past the chapel. *Av. Claude-Vellefaux.*

Turn left onto Rue de la Grange aux Belles and note the spot where the Montfauchon gibbet (or gallows) once stood. Erected in 1233 and used for nearly 400 years, the macabre structure served as a place to execute criminals and display their hanging corpses. Then, turn right onto Quai de Jemmapes.

An iron footbridge on the Canal Saint-Martin.

The rotunda on Place Stalingrad, at the start of Canal de l'Ourcq.

3 L'Hôtel du Nord. Director Marcel Carné's 1938 film Hôtel du Nord made this building (which still has its original facade) famous. Today, it's a bistro serving hearty French cuisine with a typical 1930s interior—a fine address for a spot of lunch. *102 quai de Jemmapes, 10th.* ☎ *01-40-40-78-78. www.hotel-dunord.org. $$.*

Cross back over the Canal onto Quai de Valmy.

4 ★ Quai de Valmy shops. New boutiques keep appearing along this stretch of the canal (and along adjacent Rue de Lancry and Rue Récollets). The best ones are **Artazart,** on Quai de Valmy (no. 83; ☎ 01-40-40-24-00), a cutting-edge bookshop stocking glossy publications on fashion, art, and design. Farther up, at no. 93, you'll find girly designer offerings by **Sandro** (☎ 01-46-07-05-70) , and next door at no. 95, kitsch clothes and collectables by **Antoine & Lili** (☎ 01-40-37-41-55). On Rue de Lancry, don't miss **Chez Chiffons** (no. 47;

☎ 06-64-26-11-98), the latest hot spot for affordable ladies' vintage designer apparel.

5 Bassin de la Villette. At the top of the Canal Saint-Martin, you reach the circular Barrière de la Villette, one of the few remaining 18th-century tollhouses designed by Nicolas Ledoux. The modernist fountains in front channel your view up the Canal de l'Ourcq past the twin MK2 art-house cinema complex. If you're a film buff, spend a few moments in the MK2's specialized bookshop (Quai de la Loire,19th). If you fancy a film in English, look out for VO *(version originale)* written next to the title (providing it's an English-language film, of course!).

Walk northward along the Canal de l'Ourcq.

6 Canal de l'Ourcq. Created in 1813 by Napoleon to provide drinking water and haulage, this stretch is now characterized by 1960s and '70s tower blocks. It is separated from the Bassin de la Villette by an unusual 1885 hydraulic lifting bridge.

7 Bar Ourcq. Cheap drinks make this a popular bar with residents, especially on a hot day, when boules can be hired at the bar for a game of pétanque on the sand in front of the door. Be daring and challenge a local to a game. *68 quai de la Loire, 19th.* ☎ *01-42-40-12-26. $.*

8 kids ★★★ Parc de la Villette. The city's former abattoir district is now a vast retro-futurist park with wide-open lawns and play areas for children. On site is also the excellent Cité des Sciences museum (☎ 01-40-05-70-00; www.cite-sciences.fr), with a section entirely dedicated to kids (Cité des Enfants); the Cité de la Musique music museum and concert hall (☎ 01-44-84-44-84; www.cite-musique.fr; p 134); the Zenith concert hall (www.le-zenith.com), where international bands play; and the Geode 3D-IMAX movie theater, whose silver dome sparkles in the

A barge on the Canal de l'Ourcq.

sunlight. In August, the park becomes a great outdoor cinema *(cinéma en plein-air)* with Europe's biggest inflatable screen. *Av. Corentin-Cariou, 19th.* ☎ *01-40-03-75-75. www.villette.com. Métro: Porte de la Villette or Porte de Pantin.*

The Géode in the Parc de la Villette.

Montparnasse

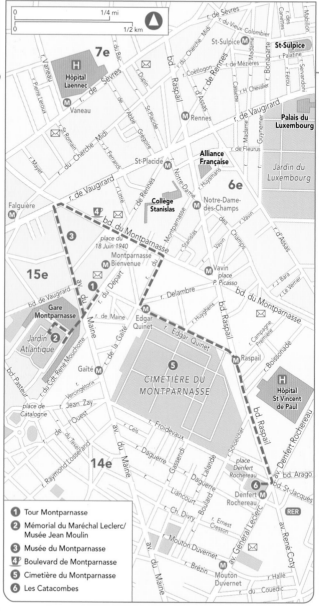

1. Tour Montparnasse
2. Mémorial du Maréchal Leclerc/ Musée Jean Moulin
3. Musée du Montparnasse
4. Boulevard de Montparnasse
5. Cimetière du Montparnasse
6. Les Catacombes

When Montmartre artists did their jobs so well that the neighborhood became popular and rents finally went up, they all moved to Montparnasse. Before long, Picasso, Léger, and Chagall had joined Man Ray, Henry Miller, and Gertrude Stein on its somewhat forbidding streets. In terms of beauty, the two areas don't compare—concrete is abundant in Montparnasse, but it offers plenty of sights to keep you busy. START: **Métro to Montparnasse-Bienvenüe.**

The view from the 56th floor of the Tour Montparnasse.

① kids ★ Tour Montparnasse.
Completed in 1973 and rising 210m (689 ft.) above the skyline, Paris's most famous inner-city skyscraper was denounced by some as "bringing Manhattan to Paris." The city soon outlawed any further structures of this size in the heart of Paris. Today, it is frequented for its panoramic viewing platform on the 56th floor, which affords the best views over the whole city. Feel your ears pop as you go up in the elevator before splurging on a cocktail or dinner in the touristy Ciel de Paris Restaurant (☎ 01-40-64-77-64), famed for its views. *33 av. de Maine, 15th. ☎ 01-45-38-52-56. www.tourmontparnasse56.com. Admission 14€ adults, 11€ ages 16–20, 8€ ages 7–15, free for children 6 & under. Apr–Sept daily 9:30am–11:30pm; Oct–Mar Sun–Thurs 9:30am–10:30pm, Fri–Sat & eve of public holidays 9:30am–11pm. Last lift 30 min. before closing. Métro: Montparnasse-Bienvenüe.*

② Mémorial du Maréchal Leclerc/Musée Jean Moulin.
This rooftop museum fills you in on World War II France and the French Resistance. The absorbing film

The Tour Montparnasse inspired a law against additional skyscrapers in the center of Paris.

archives and the art—which includes posters exhorting residents of occupied France to work in Germany—show what the French endured. ⏰ *1 hr. 23 allée de la 2e DB Jardin Atlantique (above Grandes Lignes de Gare Montparnasse), 15th.* ☎ *01-40-64-39-44. www.ml-leclerc-moulin.paris.fr. Admission 4€ adults, 2€ ages 14–26, free for children 13 & under. Tues–Sun 10am–6pm. Métro: Montparnasse- Bienvenüe.*

❸ Musée de Montparnasse.

This small gallery, located down a pretty cobbled lane, feels like a secret. It used to be an atelier/canteen frequented by Picasso, Modigliani, and other artists. Nowadays, it hosts interesting temporary art exhibitions by artists from around the world. *21 av. du Maine, 15th.* ☎ *01-42-22-91-96. www.museedu montparnasse.net. Admission 6€ adults, 5€ students, free for children under 12. Tues–Sun 12:30pm–7pm. Métro: Montparnasse or Edgar Quinet.*

❹ Boulevard du Montparnasse.

Just a block from the train station, this well-traveled street gets busiest at night, when its brasseries and cinemas are aglow, but at any time of day the enticing aromas may lure you to one of its many creperies or brasseries. Succumb to a full meal at no.108, Le Dôme, now a seafood restaurant ($$); or at no.102, La Coupole, a fabulous Art Deco brasserie ($$); or, a bit farther along, at no. 171, La Closerie des Lilas, which includes among its former fans an unlikely combination of Picasso, Trotsky, Lenin, and Hemingway ($$$).

❺ ★ Cimetière du Montparnasse.

A short walk down Boulevard Edgar-Quinet, past its many attractive cafes, takes you to this well-known burial ground. For literary and philosophical types, it's a must-see, with the graves of Samuel Beckett,

Charles Baudelaire, and Man Ray as well as the shared grave of Simone de Beauvoir and Jean-Paul Sartre, usually covered in tiny notes of intellectual affection from fans. *3 bd. Edgar-Quinet, 14th.* ☎ *01-44-10-86-50. There's a map posted to the left of the main gate. Free admission. Mon–Fri 8am–6pm, Sat 8:30am–6pm, Sun 9am–6pm. Métro: Edgar Quinet.*

❻ ★★ kids Les Catacombes.

Just before the Revolution, Paris's cemeteries were bursting at the seams, spreading disease. To solve the problem, millions of bones were transferred underground into the quarried tunnels that sprawl beneath the Denfert Rochereau district. These Catacombes, 18m (60 feet) underground, can be visited today. It feels incredibly strange seeing miles of neatly stacked bones and skulls, and it's surprisingly rather moving. The sign at the appropriately eerie entrance reads "STOP! THIS IS THE EMPIRE OF DEATH!" Older kids will love it; younger ones will probably have nightmares. ⏰ *1 hr. 1 place Denfert Rochereau, 14th.* ☎ *01-43-22-47-63. www.catacombes. paris.fr. Admission 8€ ages 27 & older, 6€ ages 14–26, free for children 13 & under. Tues–Sun 10am–5pm (last ticket sold at 4pm). Métro/RER: Denfert-Rochereau.* ●

Six million skeletons stretch 910m (2,986 ft.) through underground tunnels in Les Catacombes beneath Paris.

Shopping Best Bets

Best **Department Store**
Le Bon Marché, *22–24 rue de Sèvres, 7th (p 84)*

Best **Flea Market**
Marché aux Puces de St-Ouen, *Rue des Rosiers, 94300 Saint-Ouen (p 82)*

Best **Contemporary Art**
★ Art Generation, *67 rue de la Verrerie, 4th (p 82)*

Best **Art Supplies**
★ Viaduc des Arts, *9–147 av. Daumesnil, 12th (p 82)*

Best **Children's Clothing**
★ Bonpoint, *6 rue de Tournon, 6th (p 83)*

Best **Toy Store**
Au Nain Bleu, *5 bd. Malesherbes, 8th (p 83)*

Best **Place to Buy a Picnic Lunch**
★★★ Poilâne, *8 rue du Cherche-Midi, 6th (p 87)*

Best **Jewelry**
★★ Cartier, *23 place Vendôme, 1st (p 87)*

Best **Kitchenware**
E. Dehillerin, *18 rue Coquillière, 2nd (p 88)*

Best **Vintages Wines**
Ryst Dupeyron, *79 rue du Bac, 7th (p 87)*

Best **Place for English-Language Books & Magazines**
Galignani, *224 rue de Rivoli, 1st (p 82)*

Best **Place for Gifts**
★ Deyrolle, *45 rue du Bac, 7th (p 88)*

Best **Gourmet Food**
★ Fauchon, *26–30 place de la Madeleine, 8th (p 86)*

Best **Porcelain**
★★ Manufacture Nationale de Sèvres, *4 place André Malraux, 1st (p 84)*

Best **Place for a Princess**
Chez Chiffons, *47 rue de Lancry, 10th (p 85)*

Best **Place for a Makeover**
Makeup Me, *12 rue Montmorency, 3rd (p 88)*

Previous page: Le Bon Marché is Paris's oldest department store, from 1852.
Below: The Passage Jouffroy, one of the city's 19th-century shopping arcades.

Right Bank (8th & 16th–17th)

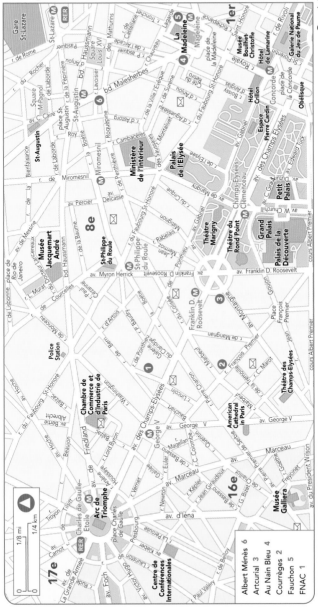

Albert Ménès 6
Artcurial 3
Au Nain Bleu 4
Courrèges 2
Fauchon 5
FNAC 1

The Best Shopping

Right Bank (1st–4th & 9th–11th)

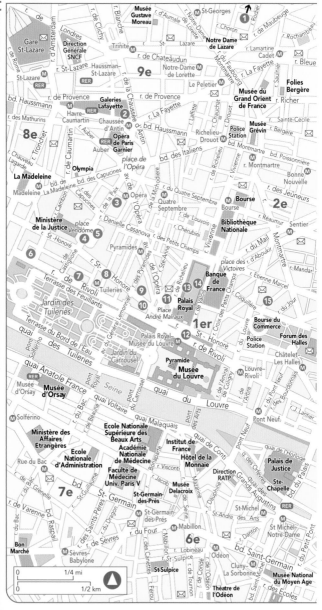

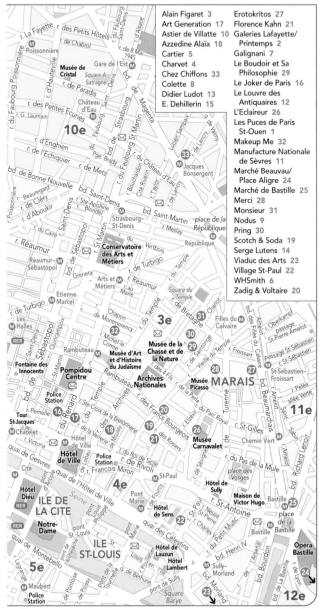

Alain Figaret 3
Art Generation 17
Astier de Villatte 10
Azzedine Alaïa 18
Cartier 5
Charvet 4
Chez Chiffons 33
Colette 8
Didier Ludot 13
E. Dehillerin 15
Erotokritos 27
Florence Kahn 21
Galeries Lafayette/
   Printemps 2
Galignani 7
Le Boudoir et Sa
   Philosophie 29
Le Joker de Paris 16
Le Louvre des
   Antiquaires 12
L'Eclaireur 26
Les Puces de Paris
   St-Ouen 1
Makeup Me 32
Manufacture Nationale
   de Sèvres 11
Marché Beauvau/
   Place Aligre 24
Marché de Bastille 25
Merci 28
Monsieur 31
Nodus 9
Pring 30
Scotch & Soda 19
Serge Lutens 14
Viaduc des Arts 23
Village St-Paul 22
WHSmith 6
Zadig & Voltaire 20

Left Bank (5th–6th)

Bonpoint 9
Deyrolle 1
Christian Constant 6
La Maison Ivre 7
Le Bon Marché 3
Librairie Michael Seksik 11
Marché Biologique 5
Poilâne 4
Ryst Dupeyron 2
Shakespeare & Company 10
Vanessa Bruno 8

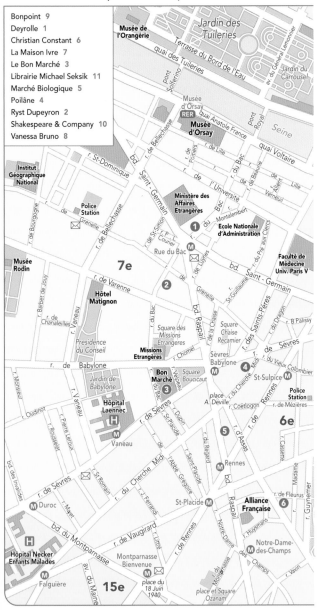

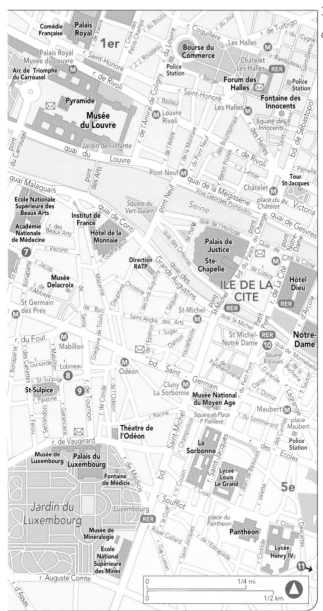

Shopping A to Z

Lighting and other housewares on display at Marché aux Puces de St-Ouen.

Antiques & Collectibles

Le Louvre des Antiquaires

PALAIS ROYAL   Across from the Louvre, this palace of antiquity is just the place if you seek 30 matching 19th-century Baccarat crystal champagne flutes or a Sèvres tea set from 1773. Its selection of jewelry and clocks absolutely sparkles. *2 place du Palais Royal, 1st.* ☎ *01-42-97-27-27. www.louvre-antiquaires. com. MC, V. Métro: Palais Royal. Map p 78.*

Marché aux Puces de St-Ouen

NORTH OF MONTMARTRE   This massive, permanent site, one of the largest flea markets in Europe, contains many 18th- and 19th-century treasures, but you'll have to haggle for them. Beware of pickpockets. *All around Rue des Rosiers in St-Ouen 94300. From the Métro, walk north along av. de la Porte de Clignancourt, (18th) then av. Michelet and turn right.* ☎ *01-40-12-32-58. www. marcheauxpuces-saintouen.com. MC, V (some stalls cash only). Métro: Porte de Clignancourt. Map p 78.*

Village St-Paul

MARAIS   This cluster of antiques and art dealers spreads across interlocking court-yards and sells quality early-20th-century furniture, bric-a-brac, and art. *23–27 rue St-Paul, 4th. No phone. www.levillagesaintpaul.com. MC, V (some boutiques cash only). Métro: St-Paul. Map p 78.*

Art

★ Artcurial CHAMPS-ELYSEES

This is the best, most prestigious place in Paris for contemporary art, from sculpture to tapestry to jewelry. *Centre d'Art Contemporain, 7 Rond-Point des Champs-Elysées, 8th.* ☎ *01-42-99-20-20. www.artcurial. com. MC, V. Métro: Franklin-D.-Roosevelt. Map p 77.*

Art Generation MARAIS

Prices here range from 60€ to 2,800€ for original, cutting-edge photographs, paintings, sculpture, video, and drawings, and who knows—the pieces you buy might be worth much more one day. *67 rue de la Verrerie, 4th.* ☎ *01-53-01-83-88. www.artgeneration.fr. MC, V. Métro: Hôtel de Ville. Map p 78.*

★ Viaduc des Arts BASTILLE

This complex of 51 boutiques and crafts shops fills the vaulted space beneath a disused 19th-century viaduct with furniture makers, potters, jewelers, and weavers. *9–147 av. Daumesnil, 12th.* ☎ *01-44-75-80-66. www.viaducdesarts.fr. Most places accept MC, V. Métro: Bastille or Gare de Lyon. Map p 78.*

Books

Galignani TUILERIES

This wood-paneled bookstore, opened in 1801, sells a vast selection of books in French and English. *224 rue de Rivoli, 1st.* ☎ *01-42-60-76-07. www. galignani.com. MC, V. Métro: Tuileries. Map p 78.*

Shakespeare & Company has long been a hub for English-speaking expats.

★★ Librairie Michael Seksik

LATIN QUARTER   This is the place to pick up literary curiosities, from 1930s editions of *Robin Hood* to '70s make-your-own paper airplane kits. There's a beautiful range of vintage photography books too. *8 rue Lacépède, 5th.* ☎ *01-43-43-53-53. www.librairiemichaelseksik.com. Métro: Place Monge. Map p 80.*

★★★ Shakespeare & Company

LATIN QUARTER   The most famous bookstore in Paris was, in its early days, a hangout for Hemingway and Fitzgerald among others. Expats still gather here to swap books and catch readings. *37 rue de la Bucherie, 5th.* ☎ *01-43-25-40-93. www.shakespeareandcompany.com. No credit cards. Métro: Maubert-Mutualité. Map p 80.*

★★ WHSmith

CONCORDE   Come to this English-language bookshop for British and American bestsellers and classics. The upstairs kids' area is an Ali Baba's cavern of fairy stories, teen lit, and games. And you can load up on BBC TV series in the DVD section. *248 rue de Rivoli, 1st.* ☎ *01-44-77-88-99. www.whsmith.fr. MC, V. Métro: Concorde. Map p 78.*

Children's Fashion & Toys

Au Nain Bleu MADELEINE   The old-world "Blue Dwarf" has been selling toys since 1836. You'll find teddies, dolls, pirate ships, and wooden puppets. *5 bd. Malesherbes, 8th.* ☎ *01-42-65-20-20. http:// boutique.aunainbleu.com. AE, MC, V. Métro: Madeleine. Map p 77.*

★ Bonpoint

CONCORDE   This place borders on haute couture for kids, so be warned. The diminutive outfits—presented in a stately 18th-century mansion—are tailored, traditional, and expensive. *6 rue de Tournon, 6th.* ☎ *01-40-51-98-20. www.bonpoint.com. AE, MC, V. Métro: Odéon. Map p 80.*

Le Joker de Paris MARAIS   Fun for adults as well as kids, this tiny boutique is packed to the gills with board games, toy soldiers, card tricks, puzzles, chess sets, and even dart boards. *77 rue de la Verrerie, 4th.* ☎ *01-42-71-21-25. www. lejokerdeparis.fr. MC, V. Métro: Hôtel de Ville. Map p 78.*

China & Porcelain

★ Astier de Villatte

PALAIS ROYAL   This space once housed Napoleon's silversmith. Nowadays,

A marionette from Au Nain Bleu.

it sells top-of-the-line handmade tableware and knickknacks inspired by 17th- and 18th-century designs. *173 rue St-Honoré, 1st.* ☎ *01-42-60-74-13. www.astierdevillatte.com. MC, V. Métro: Palais-Royal. Map p 78.*

La Maison Ivre ST-GERMAIN-DE-PRES   Handmade country-style pottery fills this adorable kitchenware shop. There's an emphasis on Provençal and artisanal ceramics. *38 rue Jacob, 6th.* ☎ *01-42-60-01-85. www.maison-ivre.com. MC, V. Métro: St-Germain-des-Prés. Map p 80.*

★★ **Manufacture Nationale de Sèvres** PALAIS ROYAL   This is where the porcelain giant Sèvres sells the plates off which kings and

Colette sells music, housewares, and art alongside designer clothing.

presidents dine. *4 place André Malraux, 1st.* ☎ *01-47-03-40-20. www. sevresciteceramique.fr. MC, V. Métro: Palais Royal. Map p 78.*

Concept & Department Stores
Colette LOUVRE   This swank fashion citadel carries men's and women's apparel by some of the city's most promising young talent, in addition to music, housewares, and art. It's for sophisticated shoppers with high credit-card limits. For a reprieve, try the excellent downstairs water bar. *213 rue St-Honoré, 1st.* ☎ *01-55-35-33-90. www.colette.fr. AE, MC, V. Métro: Tuileries or Pyramides. Map p 78.*

Galeries Lafayette/Printemps OPERA   Although separate entities, these department stores with Art Nouveau cupolas stand like twin temples to shopping along the Boulevard Haussmann. Galeries Lafayette stocks more than 90 designers and has a sumptuous food gallery (Lafayette Gourmet). Printemps has a vast shoe department (more than 200 brands) and six floors of both mid-range and designer fashion. *Galeries Lafayette: 40 bd. Haussmann, 9th.* ☎ *09-69-39-75-75. www. galerieslafayette.com. AE, MC, V. Printemps: 64 bd. Haussmann, 9th.* ☎ *01-42-82-50-00. www.printemps. com. AE, MC. Métro for both: Opéra or Chausée d'Antin Lafayette. RER: Auber. Map p 78.*

★ **Le Bon Marché** INVALIDES   Paris's oldest department store is jammed with luxury boutiques, such as Dior and Chanel, for both men and women. If you grow weary of the clothes, the Grande Epicerie food hall will dazzle you. *22–24 rue de Sèvres, 7th.* ☎ *01-44-39-80-00. www.lebonmarche.fr. AE, DC, MC, V. Métro: Sèvres-Babylone. Map p 80.*

★★★ **Merci** MARAIS/BAS-TILLE   This is Paris's first ever charity concept store. Items aren't always secondhand (some clothes, furniture lines, and other items have been created especially for the shop), and prices aren't always low, but there are bargains to be had. The money raised goes to humanitarian organizations. There's also a funky cafe. *111 bd. Beaumarchais, 3rd.* ☎ *01-42-77-01-90. www.merci-merci.com. MC, V. Métro: St-Sébastien–Froissart. Map p 78.*

Fashion

Alain Figaret OPERA One of France's foremost designers of men's shirts offers a broad range of fabrics and elegant silk ties. *21 rue de la Paix, 2nd.* ☎ *01-42-65-04-99. www.alain-figaret.fr. AE, MC, V. Métro: Opéra. Map p 78.*

Galeries Lafayette's stained-glass cupola is classified as a historic monument.

Sunday Shopping

Most shops close on Sundays, except in the Marais (Métro: St-Paul), at Bercy Village (Métro: Cour St-Emilion), and in the Carousel du Louvre underneath the Louvre museum (99 rue de Rivoli; Métro: Palais Royal–Musée du Louvre).

Azzedine Alaïa MARAIS Alaïa is known for bringing body consciousness back to French fashion (as if it had ever left). If you can't swing the price tags, try the stock shop around the corner at 18 rue de Verrerie. *7 rue de Moussy, 4th.* ☎ *01-42-72-19-19. MC, V. Métro: Hôtel-de-Ville. Map p 78.*

Charvet OPERA Charvet made shirts for fashionable Frenchmen for years before he was discovered by English royalty. (The company now makes shirts for Prince Charles.) Shop here for crisp men's and women's designs in lush fabrics. *28 place Vendôme, 1st.* ☎ *01-42-60-30-70. www.charvet.com. MC, V. Métro: Opéra. Map p 78.*

Chez Chiffons CANAL ST-MARTIN This small boutique offers exceptional vintage pieces by luxury designers, plus one-off items by lesser-known brands. *47 rue de Lancry, 10th.* ☎ *06-64-26-11-98. www.chezchiffons.fr. MC, V. Métro: Jacques Bonsergent. Map p 78.*

Courrèges CONCORDE White go-go boots, silver disco purses—here, it's the designer '70s again, with bold colors, plastic, and glitter. *40 rue François-1er, 8th.* ☎ *01-53-67-30-00. www.courreges.com. MC, V. Métro: Franklin-D.-Roosevelt. Map p 77.*

★★★ Didier Ludot PALAIS-ROYAL Recent and rare vintage haute couture and buyers with an eye for young talent (i.e., sussing out the vintage clothes of the future) make Didier Ludot exceptional. *20–24 Galerie de Montpensier, Palais Royal, 1st.* ☎ *01-42-96-06-56. www.didierludot.fr. MC, V. Métro: Palais Royal–Musée du Louvre. Map p 78.*

Erotokritos BASTILLE/MARAIS This small boutique offers trendy men's and women's fashions with a fun, eccentric edge: Think puffy

The proceeds from goods sold at Merci benefit children's charities.

gingham skirts and schoolboy-style men's shorts. *109 bd Beaumarchais, 3rd.* ☎ *01-42-78-14-04. www. erotokritos.com. MC, V. Métro: St-Sébastien Froissart. Map p 78.*

Fashion: Parisian-Style Dressing
L'Eclaireur MARAIS This futuristic-looking boutique stocks the likes of Dries Van Noten, Comme des Garçons, and Carpe Diem, as well as exclusive one-offs by lesser-known designers. Its wild interior is worth seeing even if you don't buy. *40 rue de Sevigné, 3rd.* ☎ *01-48-87-10-22. www.leclaireur.com. MC, V. Métro: St-Paul. Map p 78.*

Nodus TUILERIES This men's shirt specialist has floor-to-ceiling displays of shirts in every color under the sun as well as a few accessories, including cuff links and ties. *274 rue St-Honoré, 1st.* ☎ *01-42-60-35-13. www.nodus.fr. AE, DC, MC, V. Métro: Tuileries. Map p 78.*

★★★ Pring MARAIS Amid minimalist art galleries and progressive designer boutiques, this women's accessories shop carries a gorgeous, rainbow-hued array of sexy neo-Cinderella shoes and matching purses. A dream. *29 rue Charlot, 3rd.* ☎ *01-42-72-71-87. www.pring paris.com. Métro: Saint-Sébastien-Froissart. Map p 78.*

Scotch & Soda MARAIS Hippie-chic ethnic-print jackets, pastel

tie-dye T-shirts, and floaty floral-print dresses: This store sells women's daywear with just enough attitude to be carried into the evening. *42 rue Vieille du Temple, 4th.* ☎ *01-42-71-02-67. www.scotch-soda.com. MC, V. Métro: St-Paul. Map p 78.*

Vanessa Bruno SAINT-GERMAIN-DES-PRES Bruno's unique clothes are deeply feminine without being frilly. Her years in Japan gave her an appreciation for sleek lines and simple, clean fabrics. Great bags, too. *25 rue St-Sulpice, 6th.* ☎ *01-43-54-41-04. www.vanessa bruno.com. AE, DC, MC, V. Métro: Odéon. Map p 80.*

Zadig & Voltaire MARAIS This is one of several Z&V branches in Paris. Shelves are stocked with hip clothes in classic styles for men and women. Cotton tops, cashmere sweaters, and faded jeans are big sellers. *42 rue des Francs-Bourgeois, 3rd.* ☎ *01-44-54-00-60. www.zadig-et-voltaire.com. AE, MC, V. Métro: St-Paul or Hôtel-de-Ville. Map p 78.*

Food & Drink
Albert Ménès MADELEINE One of Paris's most prestigious small-scale purveyors of foodstuffs prides itself on selling only goods that were picked, processed, and packaged by hand. Everything from sugared almonds to terrines, Breton sardines, jams, pâtés, and more. *41 bd. Malesherbes, 8th.* ☎ *01-42-66-95-63. www.albert menes.fr. MC, V. Métro: St-Augustin or Madeleine. Map p 77.*

Christian Constant LATIN QUARTER Chocoholics rejoice. The chocolates at this divine shop are made with exotic ingredients and sold by the kilo. *37 rue d'Assas, 6th.* ☎ *01-53-63-15-15. No credit cards. Métro: St-Placide. Map p 80.*

★ Fauchon MADELEINE This fabulous upscale megadelicatessen will fill your stomach as fast as it empties your wallet. Must be seen to be believed. *26–30 place de la Madeleine, 8th.* ☎ *01-70-39-38-00. www.fauchon.com. MC, V. Métro: Madeleine. Map p 77.*

★ **Florence Kahn** MARAIS   This Jewish bakery, one of the best in the city, has all the heavy cakes, poppy seeds, apples, and cream cheese you could want. *24 rue des Ecouffes, 4th.* ☎ *01-48-87-92-85. www.florence-kahn.fr. No credit cards. Métro: St-Paul. Map p 78.*

★★★ **Poilâne** ST-GERMAIN-DES-PRES   One of the city's best-loved bakeries, with irresistible apple tarts, butter cookies, and crusty croissants. Get in line. *8 rue du Cherche-Midi, 6th.* ☎ *01-45-48-42-59. www.poilane.fr. MC, V. Métro: St-Sulpice. Map p 80.*

★★★ **Ryst Dupeyron** ST-GERMAIN-DES-PRES   Fill up on vintage wines and specialty whiskies in this family-run gem of a liquor store founded in 1905. Gourmet treats, such as foie gras and prunes in brandy, and friendly service complete the experience.*79 rue du Bac, 7th.* ☎ *01-45-48-80-93, www.maisonrystdupeyron.com. MC, V. Métro: Rue du Bac. Map p 80.*

Food & Drink: Markets
Marché Beauvau/Aligre LEDRU ROLLIN   The Marché d'Aligre is one of Paris's cheapest fruit, vegetable, and flower markets—and one of the best (Tues–Sun 7am–2pm). The more expensive, covered Marché Beauvau offers uncompromisingly good meat, fish, and cheese. *Place d'Aligre, 12th. Cash only. Métro: Ledru-Rollin. Map p 78.*

Marché Biologique SAINT-GERMAIN   Along Boulevard Raspail, this organic market (Sun 9am–3pm) sells top-notch produce, often locally sourced, plus hot soups, crêpes, and oysters to go. *Bd. Raspail (between rue du Cherche-Midi and Rue de Rennes), 6th. Cash only. Métro: Rennes. Map p 80.*

★★ **Marché de Bastille** BASTILLE   This huge market (Thurs 7:30am–2:30pm; Sun 7am–3pm) is an excellent source for local cheese, meat, and fresh fish. Street performers usually liven up the experience. *Bd. Richard Lenoir, 11th. Cash only. Métro: Bastille. Map p 78.*

Gifts & Jewelry
★★ **Cartier** CONCORDE   One of the most famous jewelers in the world, Cartier has glamorous gems to match its sky-high prices. *23 place Vendôme, 1st.*

Beneath the covered stalls of the Marché Beauvau on Place Aligre.

☎ 01-44-55-32-20. www.cartier.fr. AE, MC, V. Métro: Opéra or Tuileries. Map p 78.

★★★ Deyrolle SAINT-GERMAIN This taxidermy/curiosity shop is filled with stuffed wildlife. The chances of you leaving with a tiger in your bag are slim, but there are oodles of nature books, garden gadgets, and jewelry. The butterfly cabinets upstairs are particularly dazzling. 45 rue du Bac, 7th. ☎ 01-42-22-32-31. www.deyrolle.com. MC, V. Métro: Rue du Bac. Map p 80.

Le Boudoir et Sa Philosophie MARAIS This boudoir-themed shop sells gifts plus such eccentricities as portraits of dogs in human clothes. Bring a photo of your own Fido and commission a portrait. 18 rue Charlot, 3rd. ☎ 01-48-04-89-79. www.leboudoiretsaphilosophie.fr. MC, V. Métro: St Sébastien Froissart. Map p 78.

Monsieur MARAIS In this tiny jewelry shop, creator Nadia Azoug concocts striking unisex gold and silver bands and chains. Sometimes

All the produce is organic at Marché Biologique in Saint-Germain.

you can even watch the jewelry being made. 53 rue Charlot. ☎ 01-42-71-12-65. www.monsieur-paris.com. MC, V. Métro: Filles du Calvaire. Map p 78.

Kitchen
E. Dehillerin LES HALLES This shop has outfitted great chefs for nearly 2 centuries. Nothing here comes cheap, but a Dehillerin sauté pan is forever. 18 rue Coquilliére, 1st. ☎ 01-42-36-53-13. www.e-dehillerin.fr. MC, V. Métro: Les Halles. Map p 78.

Music & Tickets
FNAC CHAMPS-ELYSEES This supermarket of culture (with various branches) is where you can pick up CDs and vinyl of French and international artists, DVDs, video games, and electronics. It's also a convenient place to buy tickets for concerts, plays, sports events, and museums, both inside the stores and online at www.fnac.com. The branch on the Champs-Elysées stays open until midnight. 74 av. des Champs Elysées, 8th. ☎ 08-25-02-00-02. AE, DC, MC, V. Métro: George V. Map p 77.

Perfume & Makeup
Makeup Me MARAIS Stop by for a makeover on the go: This is Paris's coolest makeup bar (8€/10 min.). If you fancy a group session with the girls before a night out, book in advance, especially on weekends. 12 rue Montmorency, 3rd. ☎ 09-83-38-40-72. www.makeupme.fr. MC, V. Métro: Rambuteau. Map p 78.

★★★ Serge Lutens PALAIS ROYAL This purple Belle Epoque boutique is so beautiful it's worth seeing even if you don't buy any fragrances or makeup. This is one of a handful of boutiques to sell Lutens's "exclusives" perfume range. 142 galerie de Valois, 1st. ☎ 01-49-27-09-09. www.serge lutens.com. AE, MC, V. Métro: Palais Royal. Map p 78. ●

Jardin des Tuileries

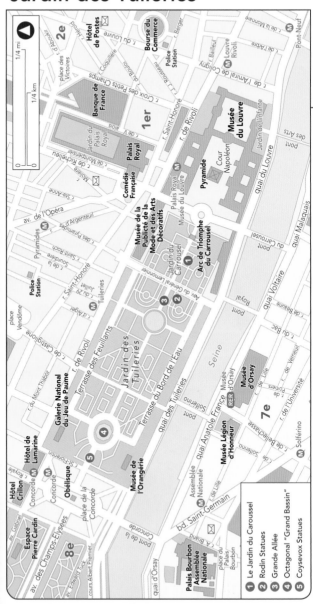

1 Le Jardin du Caroussel
2 Rodin Statues
3 Grande Allée
4 Octagonal "Grand Bassin"
5 Coysevox Statues

Previous page: Sculpture in the Jardin des Tuileries.

More a statue garden than, as its name implies, a "garden of tiles" (the clay earth here was once used to make roof tiles), the Tuileries stretches from the Louvre all the way down to the Place de la Concorde. Under lacy chestnut trees, paths branch and curl off the dusty main allée, and each seems to hold something to charm you—statues, ice-cream stands, and ponds surrounded by chairs you can move to the water's edge in which to read or contemplate the beauty around you. It's open daily from 7am to 9pm in summer and from 7am to 5:45pm in winter. START: **Métro to Tuileries or Concorde.**

❶ **Le Jardin du Carrousel.** Start by the glass pyramid and walk past the Arc de Triomphe du Carrousel—a lesser yet still quite elaborate arch ordered by Napoleon in 1806 and copied from the Septimus Severus Arch in Rome—into the eastern edge of the Tuileries, the Jardin du Carrousel. (Just so you know, the last word refers to equestrian exhibitions—there's no merry-go-round here.) The gold-tipped obelisk you see gleaming at the end (the Luxor Obelisk, a gift from Egypt) marks the Place de la Concorde. As you walk into the garden, you'll pass street vendors hawking cheap imported Eiffel Towers—poor copies of the real deal visible beyond the treetops. But look around and you'll find beautiful boxwood hedges, among which 20 graceful statues by Aristide Maillol seemingly play hide and seek.

❷ **Rodin Statues.** Extricate yourself from the crowds and keep walking until you cross Avenue du Général-Lemonnier. Four typically graceful statues by Auguste Rodin (*The Kiss, Eve, Meditation,* and *The Shadow*) flank the paths. The glimmering golden statue in the distance at Place des Pyramides is *Joan of Arc;* she assembled her army against the British from a spot not far from here, on Avenue de l'Opéra.

❸ **Grande Allée.** Off to the sides of the Grande Allée, a number of modern statues peek at you from the greenery—Henry Moore's *Figure Couchée* lounges leisurely, and

The Grand Bassin in the Jardin des Tuileries is surrounded by statues.

Alberto Giacometti's *Grande Femme II* sits near Jean Dubuffet's dazzling *Le Bel Costume.* Particularly beguiling is *The Welcoming Hands*—a collage of intertwined hands, by Louise Bourgeois.

❹ **Octagonal "Grand Bassin."** The statues surrounding this pond date from the days when this was a royal park fronting the ill-fated Palais Tuileries, which burned to the ground during a battle in 1871. But the area's layout has changed little since André Le Nôtre, Louis XIV's landscape architect, first designed it in the 17th century. The statues are all allegories—of the seasons, French rivers, the Nile, and the Tiber.

❺ **Coysevox Statues.** At the end of the garden, at the gates facing the Place de la Concorde, are copies of a set of elaborate statues originally created by Charles-Antoine Coysevox (1640–1720), one of Louis XIV's sculptors. They depict the gods Mercury and Fame riding winged horses.

Cimetière du Père-Lachaise

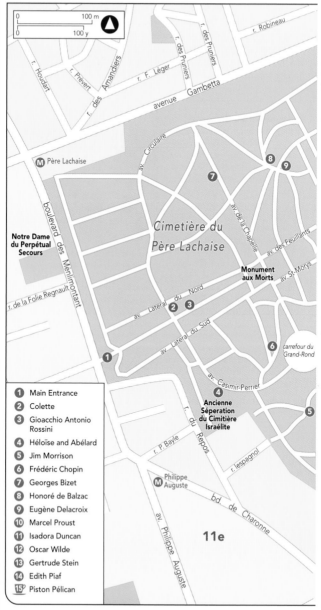

1 Main Entrance

2 Colette

3 Gioacchio Antonio Rossini

4 Héloïse and Abélard

5 Jim Morrison

6 Frédéric Chopin

7 Georges Bizet

8 Honoré de Balzac

9 Eugène Delacroix

10 Marcel Proust

11 Isadora Duncan

12 Oscar Wilde

13 Gertrude Stein

14 Edith Piaf

15° Piston Pélican

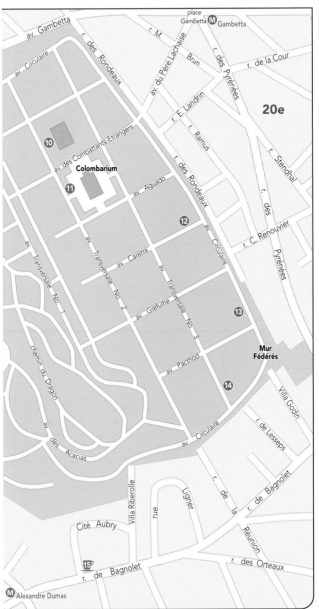

av. Gambetta

r. des Rondeaux

r. M.

av. du Père-Lachaise

Brun

r. des Pyrénées

r. de la Cour

av. Circulaire

r. E. Landrin

20e

r. Ramus

r. Stendhal

⑩

av. des Combattants-Etrangers

r. des Rondeaux

r. des

Colombarium

av. Aguado

r. C. Renouvier

⑪

av. Circulaire

⑫

Pyrénées

av. Transversale No. 1

av. Transversale No. 2

av. Carette

av. Transversale No. 3

av. Grefulhe

⑬

chemin du Dragon

av. Pacthod

Mur
Fédérés

⑭

av. des Acacias

av. Circulaire

Villa Godin

r. de Lesseps

r. de la

Villa Riberolle

rue

Ligner

r. de Bagnolet

Cité Aubry

Réunion

⑮

r. de Bagnolet

r. des Orteaux

Ⓜ Alexandre Dumas

Père-Lachaise became one of the world's most famous cemeteries when Jim Morrison died (or didn't die, as some fans believe), in 1971. Almost immediately, Morrison's grave became a site of pilgrimage and the place filled with tourists, most of whom you can avoid if you stay away from Morrison's grave. Aside from its VIP RIPs, Père Lachaise is a peaceful place to get away from the hubbub of city life. It's also a magnet for lovers of sculpture, who can admire some of Europe's most intricate and beautiful 19th-century tombstones. START: **Métro to Philippe-Auguste or Père Lachaise.**

The city acquired the cemetery in 1804; 19th-century sculpture abounds.

1 Main Entrance. Start by picking up a free map at the gate. *Bd. de Ménilmontant & Rue de la Roquette.* ☎ *01-55-25-82-10. Free admission. Daily 8:30am (9am Sun & public holidays) to 6pm (until 5:30pm in winter). Métro: Philippe-Auguste or Père-Lachaise.*

2 Colette. French writer Sidonie-Gabrielle Colette published 50 novels. Her most famous story, *Gigi,* became a successful Broadway play and film. When she died in 1954, she was given a state funeral but was refused Roman Catholic rites because of her naughty lifestyle. *Section 4.*

3 Gioacchio Antonio Rossini. The Italian composer is best known for the operas *The Barber of Seville* and *William Tell,* the overture of which is one of the most famous in

the world. His dramatic style led to his nickname among other composers—"Monsieur Crescendo." *Section 4.*

4 Héloïse & Abelard. If you turn right down Avenue du Puits, near Colette's grave, you'll soon come to the oldest inhabitants of the cemetery. These star-crossed medieval lovers were kept apart their entire lives by Héloïse's family. Their passionate love letters to one another were published and have survived the ages. Abelard died first. Local lore maintains that when Héloïse died, a romantic abbess opened Abelard's grave to put Héloïse's body inside, and his corpse opened its arms to embrace his long-lost love. *Section 7.*

5 Jim Morrison. If you must visit Morrison's grave, follow the crowds. The bust that once stood at the head of the tomb was stolen years ago by one of his "fans." The cigarette butts stubbed out on the grave are also courtesy of his "fans." As are the graffiti and the stench of old beer. What a mess. *Section 6.*

6 Frédéric Chopin. Retrace your steps across Avenue Casimir-Périer to section 11, where you'll find the elaborate grave of the piano maestro marked with a statue of Erato, the muse of music. *Section 11.*

7 Georges Bizet. The 19th-century composer of the impossibly infectious opera *Carmen* died 3 months after the premiere of his most famous work, convinced it was a failure. *Section 68.*

8 Honoré de Balzac. The passionate French novelist wrote for up to 15 hours a day, drinking prodigious quantities of coffee to keep him going. His writing was often sloppy and uninspired, but it makes an excellent record of 19th-century Parisian life. *Section 48.*

9 Eugène Delacroix. This dramatic and intensely romantic painter's *Liberty Leading the People* is a lesson in topless inspiration. In stark contrast, his tomb is sobriety incarnate: just a dark stone sculpture, shaped like a coffin and decorated with a single row of white-centered flowers. *Section 49.*

10 Marcel Proust. The wistful 19th-century novelist died before he could finish editing his famous series of books, *A la Recherche du Temps Perdu (In Search of Lost Time)*, yet he's considered one of the world's great writers. *Section 85.*

11 Isadora Duncan. The tragic death of this marvelous modern dancer is legendary—she favored long, dramatic scarves and convertibles, and one day one of those wrapped around the other and that was the end of Isadora. *Section 87.*

12 Oscar Wilde. The bluntly named Avenue des Etrangers Morts pour la France (Avenue of Dead Foreigners, basically) leads to the fantastical tomb of this gay 19th-century wit and writer. The size of the member with which the statue atop the grave was equipped was quite the buzz in Paris until a vengeful woman knocked it off. *Section 89.*

13 Gertrude Stein. The early-20th-century writer, art collector, and unlikely muse shares a simple double-sided tomb with her long-time companion, Alice B. Toklas. *Section 94.*

14 Edith Piaf. Just one more stop before you collapse—the resting place of famed French songbird Edith Piaf, beloved by broken-hearted lovers and gay men everywhere. *Section 97.*

15 Exit. Leave the cemetery at Rue de la Réunion, and from there head right down Rue de Bagnolet to the Alexandre Dumas Métro station. On the way, shabby-chic bar Piston et Pélican is perfect for a glass of wine alongside arty crowds. Stay after 9pm for live music. *15 rue de Bagnolet, 20th.* ☎ *01-43-71-15-76. www. pistonpelican.com. Open from 5pm.*

The tombstone of Oscar Wilde is decorated with a once-well-endowed figure.

Exploring the **Bois de Boulogne**

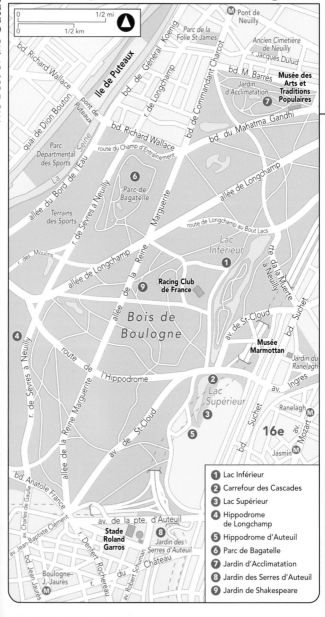

1 Lac Inférieur
2 Carrefour des Cascades
3 Lac Supérieur
4 Hippodrome de Longchamp
5 Hippodrome d'Auteuil
6 Parc de Bagatelle
7 Jardin d'Acclimatation
8 Jardin des Serres d'Auteuil
9 Jardin de Shakespeare

This former forest, once used for royal hunts, has two person-alities. By day, it's a family park where children gambol and ride ponies, while walkers and cyclists take in the beauty of its lakes and waterfalls. By night, it's one of the city's busiest prostitution districts and a hub for other nefarious activities, so make sure you get out before sundown. While you're there, however, you're in for a bucolic day amid birds, woodlands, and 19th-century tropical greenhouses. Between May and September, you can even take in classical the-ater (in English and French) among the sweet-scented roses of the Jardin de Shakespeare. START: **RER to Avenue Foch.**

1 Lac Inférieur. Most easily accessed by way of Avenue Foch, this unfairly named lake (it's the larger of the two) has two pictur-esque islands connected by fanciful footbridges. You can rent a boat and paddle across to the islands' cafes and restaurants. On a hot summer day, it's also a perfect spot for a picnic.

2 Carrefour des Cascades. The scenic walkway between the upper and lower lakes is an attrac-tion in itself, with willows dipping their branches languorously in the water, and a handsome, man-made waterfall creating a gorgeous back-drop. You can even walk under the waterfall.

3 Lac Supérieur. The smaller of the two lakes has more of every-thing you find on the larger lake, with lots of boats to paddle and several restaurants and cafes dot-ted about.

4 Hippodrome de Long-champ. If your euros are burning a hole in your pocket, head to the southern end of the park, where two horse-racing courses—the excellent Hippodrome de Long-champ and the smaller Hippo-drome d'Auteuil (see next stop)—offer galloping action. The Grand Prix held at Longchamp each June is a major derby and gets the ladies out to the track in their finest hats. *Route des Tribunes,*

Bois de Boulogne is known as the green lung of the French capital.

16th. ☎ *01-44-30-75-00. www. france-galop.com. Métro: Porte Maillot then bus 244 and get off at Carrefour de Longchamp.*

⑤ Hippodrome d'Auteuil. This racetrack, the smaller of the two in Bois de Boulogne, is known for its heart-pounding steeplechases and obstacle courses. *Route d'Auteuil aux Lacs, 16th.* ☎ *01-40-71-47-47. www.france-galop.com. Métro: Porte d'Auteuil-Hippodrome.*

⑥ Parc de Bagatelle. This romantic 18th-century park-within-a-park in the northwest of Bois de Boulogne is a riot of colorful tulips in spring, and the rose garden blooms spectacularly by late May. A sequence of little bridges, grottoes, and water features also make it one of Paris's most popular trysting spots. ☎ *01-40-67-97-00. Métro: Porte d'Auteuil or Jasmin.*

⑦ ★★ kids Jardin d'Acclimatation. Those with small children may want to head

straight to this amusement park on the north end of Bois de Boulogne, which boasts colorful rides, a small zoo, and a kid-size train. *See p 29,* ⑥.

⑧ ★★ Jardin des Serres d'Auteuil. These elegant glass-and-iron greenhouses (built in 1898 and strewn among beautifully landscaped English and Japanese gardens) are a botanist's dream, with rows of tropical plants each bigger and more colorful than the last. *1 av. Gordon Bennett, 16th.* ☎ *01-71-28-50-82. www.paris.fr. Métro: Porte d'Auteuil.*

⑨ ★★ Jardin de Shakespeare. This has to be one of the most beautiful open-air theaters in the world—a lawn encircled by bright, buzzing flowerbeds and draping trees. Every summer, it becomes the idyllic stage for Shakespeare and classical French children's theater productions. *In the Jardin Pré-Catelan. www.jardinshakespeare.fr. Métro: Porte de la Muette.* ●

Bois de Boulogne: Practical Matters

Bois de Boulogne is open daily from dawn to dusk. Because it's such a large park, there are several entrances and several public transportation options. Nearby Métro stops include Les Sablons (north, on av. Charles de Gaulle), Porte Maillot (northeast, on av. de la Grande Armée), Porte Dauphine (northeast, on av. Foch), or Porte d'Auteuil (southeast, on av. de la Porte d'Auteuil). Take the RER to Avenue Foch or Avenue Henri Martin. In the park are numerous cafes and restaurants. A miniature train runs to the Jardin d'Acclimatation from Porte Maillot—a fun touch for kids. You won't be able to do the whole of the Bois in one day, but to see a maximum of sites, bikes can be hired near the Jardin d'Acclimatation and the Lac Inférieur (☎ 01-47-47-76-50). They cost around 10€ for half a day, and there are plenty of cycle paths to follow.

Dining **Best Bets**

Best **for Perfect Soufflés**
★ La Cigalle-Récamier $$$ *4 rue Récamier, 7th (p 109)*

Best **for High Teas**
★ Angélina $$ *226 rue de Rivoli, 1st (p 106)*

Best **for Kids**
★ Breakfast in America $
17 rue des Ecoles, 5th (p 108)

Best **Cheap Meal in 19th-Century Surroundings**
★ Chartier $ *7 rue du Faubourg Montmartre, 9th (p 108)*

Best **Comfort Food**
★★ Astier $$$ *44 rue Jean-Pierre Timbaud, 11th (p 106)*

Best **Vegetarian**
★★ Le Potager du Marais $$
22 rue Rambuteau, 3rd (p 111)

Best **Seafood**
★ Les Fables de la Fontaine $$$
131 rue St-Dominique, 7th (p 110)

Best **for a Michelin-Starred Feast**
★★★ La Dame de Pic $$$$$ *20 rue du Louvre, 1st (p 110)*

Best **Gourmet Asian**
Shangri-La $$$$$ *10 av. d'Iéna, 16th (p 112)*

Best **for Food Critics**
★★★ Le Grand Véfour $$$$$
17 rue de Beaujolais, 2nd (p 110)

Best **Bourgeois Cooking**
★ Chez Georges $$$ *1 rue du Mail, 2nd (p 108)*

Best **for Contemporary French Cuisine**
★ Septime $$$$ *80 rue de Charonne, 11th (p 112)*

Best **Cheap Lunch**
Higuma $ *32 bis rue Ste-Anne, 2nd (p 109)*

Best **Romantic Summer Splurge**
Lasserre $$$$$ *17 av. Franklin Roosevelt, 8th (p 110)*

Best **Celebrity-Chef Restaurant**
★★★ Chez Jean-François Piège $$$$$ *In the Hôtel Thoumieux, 79 rue St-Dominique, 7th (p 111)*

Best **Trendy Pizzas**
★★ Pink Flamingo $ *67 rue Bichat, 10th (p 112)*

Best **Food & Wine Pairing**
★★★ Le Grand 8 $$ *8 rue Lamarck, 18th (p 110)*

Previous page: Appetizing decor at Le Grand Véfour.
Below: Kids are always welcome at the Pink Flamingo pizza parlor.

Right Bank (8th & 16th–17th)

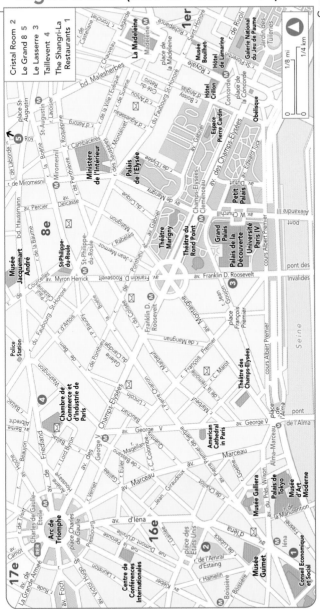

Cristal Room 2
Le Grand 8 5
Le Lasserre 3
Taillevent 4
The Shangri-La Restaurants 1

Right Bank (1st–4th & 9th–11th)

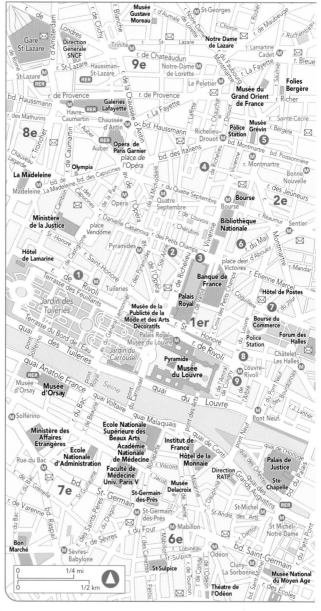

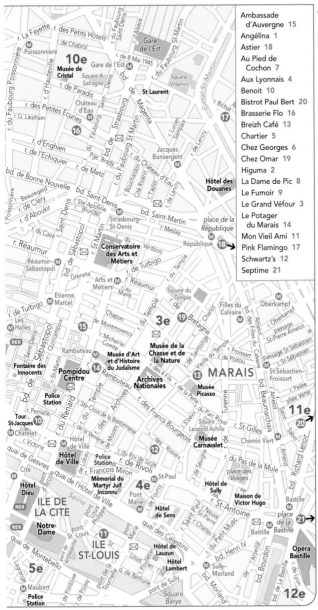

The Best Dining

Left Bank (5th–6th)

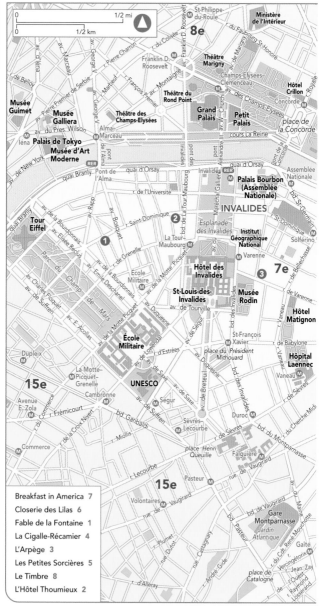

0 | 1/2 mi
0 | 1/2 km

St-Philippe-du-Roule
Ministère de l'Intérieur
8e
r. du Faubourg St-Honoré
r. de Marigny
av. Franklin D. Roosevelt
r. du Colisée
av. Pierre Charron
av. George V
av. Marceau
av. d'Iéna

Théâtre Marigny

Franklin D. Roosevelt

Champs-Elysées-Clemenceau
Hôtel Crillon
av. des Champs-Elysées
Concorde
place de la Concorde
av. W. Churchill

Théâtre du Rond Point

Grand Palais
Petit Palais
cours La Reine

av. Montaigne
av. François Premier
av. Marbeuf
av. Pierre Premier de Serbie
r. de Belloy

Musée Guimet
Musée Galliera
av. du Prés. Wilson
Théâtre des Champs-Elysées
Alma Marceau

Palais de Tokyo
Iéna
Musée d'Art Moderne
RER
av. de New York
quai Branly
Pont de l'Alma
pont de l'Alma
quai d'Orsay
Invalides RER
quai d'Orsay
place de la Concorde
pont de la Concorde
pont Alexandre III
pont des Invalides
Maréchal Gallieni

Assemblée Nationale
Palais Bourbon (Assemblée Nationale)
bd. St-Germain
r. de l'Université
r. St-Dominique
Solférino

Tour Eiffel
quai Branly
av. de la Bourdonnais
av. Elisée Reclus
Parc du Champ de Mars
av. de Suffren
av. Charles Floquet
av. Joseph Bouvard
Dupleix
av. de la Motte Picquet
r. de Grenelle
r. St-Dominique
INVALIDES
Esplanade des Invalides
Institut Géographique National
La Tour-Maubourg
av. du Maréchal Gallieni
Varenne
7e
r. de Bellechasse
r. de Varenne

1
2
r. St-Dominique
r. Saint-Dominique
av. Bosquet
École Militaire
av. de la Bourdonnais
av. Emile Deschanel

Hôtel des Invalides
St-Louis-des-Invalides
av. de Tourville
Musée Rodin
3
Hôtel Matignon
av. de Ségur
bd. des Invalides
r. de Varenne
r. Vaneau

École Militaire
av. de Lowendal
av. de la Motte Picquet
av. Duquesne
r. d'Estrées
St-François Xavier
place du Président Mithouard
av. Duquesne
Duroc
Hôpital Laennec
Vaneau
r. de Sèvres

Dupleix
av. de Suffren
La Motte-Picquet-Grenelle
UNESCO
av. de Saxe
av. de Breteuil
bd. des Invalides
r. du Cherche Midi

15e
Avenue E. Zola
r. du Commerce
r. Frémicourt
Cambronne
Ségur
av. de Saxe
bd. du Montparnasse
Falguière
r. de Vaugirard

Commerce
r. de la Croix Nivert
bd. Garibaldi
r. Miollis
Sèvres-Lecourbe
place Henri Queuille
r. de Sèvres

r. Lecourbe
15e
Pasteur
rue de Vaugirard

Volontaires
rue de Vaugirard
Gare Montparnasse
Jardin Atlantique
Gaîté
r. du Commandant René Mouchotte
r. Vercingétorix
Jean-Zay
r. de l'Ouest
r. Raymond Losserand

r. Plumet
rue du Dr. Roux
rue de Castagnary
rue André Gide
r. d'Alleray
place de Catalogne

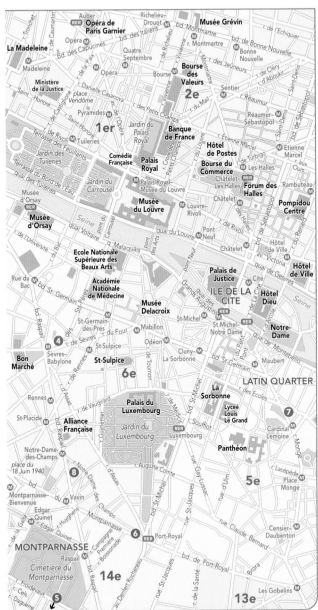

Restaurants A to Z

You're likely to catch fashion-industry mavens taking tea at Angélina.

★★ Ambassade d'Auvergne

BEAUBOURG *TRADITIONAL FRENCH* The Auvergne is a region known for its hearty cuisine. And this friendly restaurant does it justice with large tasty portions of such specials as lentils cooked in goose fat (which tastes better than it sounds), beef stewed in red wine, and rich and gooey aligot (potatoes, garlic, and cheese). *22 rue du Grenier St-Lazare, 3rd.* ☎ *01-42-72-31-22. www.ambassade-auvergne. com. Entrees 16€–24€, prix-fixe menu 31€, 3-course average 45€. MC, V. Lunch & dinner daily; July 14–Aug 15 closed Sun. Métro: Rambuteau. Map p 102.*

★ Angélina TUILERIES *TEA SHOP*

This traditional salon de thé serves its high-society patrons tea, pastries, and sandwiches on silver platters. If you have a sweet tooth, try the house special Mont Blanc, a gooey meringue, cream, and chestnut cake. The hot chocolate is one of the best in Paris too. *226 rue de Rivoli, 1st.* ☎ *01-42-60-82-00. www. angelina-paris.fr. Tea 6€–11€, entrees*

12€–18€. AE, MC, V. Breakfast, lunch & tea daily. Métro: Tuileries or Concorde. Map p 102.

★★ Astier OBERKAMPF *FRENCH*

This red-and-white-checkered dining institution is where chef Christophe Kestler reworks vintage staples, such as smoked herring and potato salad, wild-boar terrine, and braised Charolais beef, with modern flair. The staff is friendly, the wine list long, and the managers also own the next-door Italian restaurant and fine-food épicerie, so if Astier is all booked up, you won't go hungry. *44 rue Jean-Pierre Timbaud, 11th.* ☎ *01-43-57-16-35. www.restaurant-astier.com. 3-course average 35€–45€, prix-fixe menu 33€–39€. Lunch & dinner daily. MC, V. Métro: Oberkampf. Map p 102.*

★ Au Pied de Cochon.

Where else in Paris can you get such a good meal at 3am? Specialties include onion soup, grilled pigs' feet with béarnaise sauce, and *andouillettes.* On the street outside, you can buy some of the freshest oysters in town. *6 rue Coquillière,*

Diners under the vaulted arcades of the Marais district.

Au Pied de Cochon is open 24 hours.

1st. ☎ 01-40-13-77-00. www.pied-decochon.com. *Entrees 17€–48€. AE, DC, MC, V. Daily 24 hr. Métro: Les Halles or Louvre. Map p 102.*

★ **Aux Lyonnais** GRANDS BOULEVARDS *LYONNAIS* Famed chef Alain Ducasse, the best in Paris at Lyonnais cuisine, creates such dishes as parsleyed calf's liver, pike dumplings, skate meunière, and peppery coq au vin in a restaurant designed to look like a 19th-century bistro. *32 rue St-Marc, 2nd.* ☎ 01-42-96-65-04. www.alain-ducasse.com. *Reservations required. Prix-fixe menu from 32€ (lunch), 3-course average 45€. AE, DC, MC, V. Lunch & dinner Tues–Fri, dinner Sat. Métro: Grands Boulevards. Map p 102.*

★ **Benoit** MARAIS *TRADITIONAL FRENCH* Since 1912, every mayor of Paris has dined at Benoit; perhaps that explains the air of gravitas here. Time-tested classics fill the menu—my favorites are the escargot, cassoulet, and, for dessert, Sainte-Eve (pears with cream). *20 rue St-Martin, 4th.* ☎ 01-42-72-25-76. www.benoit-paris.com. *Reservations required. Entrees 24€–52€, prix-fixe lunch 38€. AE, MC, V. Lunch & dinner daily. Métro: Hôtel-de-Ville. Map p 102.*

★★★ **kids** **Bistrot Paul Bert** FAIDHERBE FRENCH This locals'

haunt has old tile floors and a real zinc bar—just as a Parisian bistro should. The food is just as authentic and delicious: crispy duck confit with garlicky potatoes, homemade pâtés, and possibly the best *île flottante* (whisked egg whites in a vanilla sauce) in town. *11 rue Paul Bert, 12th.* ☎ 01-43-72-24-01. *Entrees 24€. 3-course menu 35€–40€. MC, V. Lunch & dinner Tues–Sat. Métro: Faidherbe-Chaligny. Map p 102.*

★★ **Brasserie Flo** NORTHEAST PARIS *TRADITIONAL FRENCH* This well-known restaurant is a bit hard to find, down a discreet

Parisians flock to Bistrot Paul Bert for île flottantes, homemade pâtés, and other bistro staples in a classic setting.

Imaginative organic crepes and artisanal ciders are Breizh Café's specialties.

cobbled passage, but you'll be glad you tracked it down when you try the onion soup, sole meunière, or guinea hen with lentils. *7 cour des Petites-Ecuries, 10th.* ☎ *01-47-70-13-59. www.brasserieflo-paris. com. Reservations recommended. Entrees 20€ –40€, prix-fixe lunch & dinner 28€–33€. AE, DC, MC, V. Lunch & dinner daily. Métro: Château d'Eau or Strasbourg-St-Denis. Map p 102.*

★ kids **Breakfast in America** LATIN QUARTER *AMERICAN* Homesick Americans make a bee-line to this diner, which could have been transported here straight from the streets of Chicago. The menu features such favorites as pancakes with maple syrup, freshly squeezed OJ, burgers with grilled onions and fries, and brownies. *17 rue des Ecoles, 5th.* ☎ *01-43-54-50-28. www.breakfast-in-america.com. Entrees 8€–17€. MC, V. Breakfast, lunch & dinner daily. Métro: Cardinal Lemoine. Map p 104.*

★ kids **Breizh Café** MARAIS *CREPERIE* You could be in Brittany at this upbeat modern creperie, which uses top-notch, mostly organic produce in its unusual and delicious fillings: Think potato and smoked herring, or 70 percent cocoa solids in the chocolate dessert crêpes. You can wash it all down with one of 15 artisanal ciders. *109 rue Vieille-du-Temple,*

3rd. ☎ *01-42-72-13-77. www.breizh cafe.com. Crêpes 6€–15€. MC, V. Lunch & dinner Wed–Sun. Métro: Filles du Calvaire. Map p 102.*

★ kids **Chartier** LES HALLES *TRADITIONAL FRENCH* This unpretentious, affordable fin-de-siècle restaurant has soaring ceilings, fabulous brasswork, and straightforward cooking—try the beef bourguignon (in red-wine sauce), the pavé (thick steak), or the fish. *7 rue du Faubourg Montmartre, 9th.* ☎ *01-47-70-86-29. www.restaurant-chartier. com. Entrees 9€–14€. MC, V. Lunch & dinner daily. Métro: Grands Boulevards. Map p 102.*

★ **Chez Georges** PALAIS ROYAL *TRADITIONAL FRENCH* This restaurant welcomes you with wood paneling, elegant linen-draped tables, and the promise of timeless classics, such as *oeufs en meurette* (eggs poached in red wine). Order a glass of full-bodied red, then loosen your belt for a gut-busting portion of *entrecôte* (steak) with bone marrow or grilled kidneys with crunchy fries. The rum baba—awash in rum—is to die for. *1 rue du Mail, 2nd.* ☎ *01-42-60-07-11. Entrees 25€–45€. MC, V. Lunch & dinner Mon–Fri. Métro: Palais Royal or Sentier. Map p 102.*

★ **Chez Omar** MARAIS *NORTH AFRICAN* Fashionistas no longer line the walls of this popular shabby-chic couscous restaurant, but you should still be prepared to queue. Your patience will be rewarded with a copious—and I mean copious—portion of couscous, laden with vegetable broth, spicy merguez sausages, or lamb shoulder. Feeling hungry? Order the *couscous royal*, with all the aforementioned trimmings! *47 rue de la Bretagne, 3rd.* ☎ *01-42-72-36-26. No reservations. Entrees 13€–20€. MC, V. Lunch & dinner Mon–Sat, dinner Sun. Métro: Temple or Arts et Métiers. Map p 102.*

★ **Closerie des Lilas** MONTPAR-
NASSE *TRADITIONAL FRENCH*
This restaurant and brasserie was a
favorite of Gertrude Stein and
Picasso (not to mention Lenin and
Trotsky—a revolution marches on
its stomach, apparently). Have a
champagne julep before stuffing
yourself with veal ribs with cider or
filet of beef in peppercorn sauce.
171 bd. du Montparnasse, 6th. ☎ *01-
40-51-34-50. www.closeriedeslilas.fr.
Reservations far in advance for the
restaurant, not needed for the brasserie. Restaurant entrees 30€–50€;
brasserie entrees 25€–30€. AE, DC,
V. Lunch & dinner daily. Métro: Port
Royal or Vavin. Map p 104.*

Cristal Room CHAMPS-ELYSEES
HAUTE CUISINE You have to
climb a red carpet encrusted with
crystals to get to Baccarat's chic
dining room. Once you're inside,
chef Thomas L'Hérisson's cuisine
lives up to the grand entrance with
filets of red mullet in a chickpea and
coriander crust or perfect pan-fried
veal cutlet with tandoori gnocchi. A
meal here also includes a trip around
the tiny but stunningly beautiful
Baccarat museum. *11 place des*

*The chandelier in the Cristal Room prom-
ises more to come in the on-site Baccarat
museum.*

Etats-Unis, 16th. ☎ *01-40-22-11-10.
www.baccarat.fr. Lunch 36€–55€,
3-course menu 109€–159€ (w/ drinks).
MC, V. Lunch & dinner Mon–Sat.
Métro: Boissière or Iéna. Map p 101.*

Higuma OPERA *JAPANESE* This
no-frills Japanese canteen is always
full, so get here early if you don't
want to queue in the street at meal-
times. The reasons behind its popu-
larity are the quirky open kitchen,
which fills the air with delicious-
smelling steam, and the low prices—
around 9€ for a giant bowl of soup,
rice, or noodles, piled high with
meat, seafood, or stir-fried vegetables. If there's no room, walk 5 minutes to the sister Higuma at 163 rue
St-Honoré (1st). *32 bis rue Ste-Anne,
1st.* ☎ *01-47-03-38-59. www.
higuma.fr. Prix-fixe menu from 13€,
entrees 9€. MC, V. Lunch & dinner
daily. Métro: Pyramides. Map p 102.*

★★ **L'Arpège** INVALIDES *FRENCH*
Supplies for this exclusive eaterie
come from chef Alain Passard's
own farms in the Sarthe, Eure, and
Mont-Saint-Michel regions, where
horses replace polluting machinery,
and pesticides (when necessary) are
vegetable-based. Expect such
Michelin-starred dishes as roasted
Brittany turbot with smoked potatoes and blue lobster in honey. *84
rue de Varenne, 7th.* ☎ *01-47-05-09-
06. www.alain-passard.com. Entrees
60€–140€. AE, MC, V. Mon–Fri noon–
2:30pm & 7:30–10:30pm. Métro:
Varenne. Map p 104.*

★★ **La Cigalle-Récamier** SAINT-
GERMAIN-DES-PRES *SOUFFLES*
Whichever flavor you order, be they
savory or sweet, La Cigalle's soufflés are perfect every time, and the
most delicious in Paris. Perhaps
that's why the restaurant is favored
by the crème de la crème of Saint-
Germain society. On a sunny day,
the terrace is a special treat. Service can be unfriendly: Just shrug it
off—this is Paris. *4 rue Récamier,*

7th. ☎ 01-45-48-86-58. *Entrees 20€–45€. MC, V. Lunch & dinner Mon–Sat. Métro: Sèvres-Babylone. Map p 104.*

★★★ La Dame de Pic LOUVRE

CONTEMPORARY FRENCH Run by Michelin-starred chef Anne-Sophie Pic, this restaurant exudes savoir-faire. Choose your menu using your sense of smell: The waiters offer perfumed cards that correspond to ingredients used in the dishes. Then tuck into veal with bacon and saffron, or pigeon with rhubarb, and such desserts as strawberry and mint baba—all as photogenic as they are delicious. *20 rue du Louvre, 1st. ☎ 01-42-60-40-40. www.ladamedepic.fr. Reservations recommended. Entrees 35€–70€, prix-fixe lunch 49€, prix-fixe dinner 79€–120€. MC, V. Lunch & dinner Mon–Sat. Métro: Louvre-Rivoli. Map p 102.*

★★ Lasserre CHAMPS ELYSEES

HAUTE FRENCH Eating here with gold cutlery and fine porcelain, waiters plying to your every whim, and Michelin-starred food on your plate is a treat available to only a lucky few. If you can afford it, do it, especially in summer, when the restaurant roof opens to let in the

Low prices, an open kitchen, and delicious soups draw crowds to Higuma.

warm breeze. Lunch is less than half the price of dinner, for the same food. *17 av. Franklin Roosevelt, 8th. ☎ 01-43-59-02-13. www.restaurant-lasserre.com. Reservations recommended. Prix-fixe lunch 80€, prix-fixe dinner 195€, entrees 60€–110€. MC, V. Lunch & dinner Thurs–Fri, dinner Sat–Wed. Métro: Champs Elysée Clémenceau. Map p 101.*

★ Le Fumoir LOUVRE *BISTRO*

This handy spot near the Louvre and Arts Décoratifs museums has a faithful following from Paris's literary and media crowds. Sink into a Chesterfield armchair and order a refreshing fruit cocktail, or fill up on salads, steak, or vegetarian risotto. *6 rue de l'amiral de Coligny, 1st. ☎ 01-42-92-00-24. www.lefumoir. com. Entrees average 17€; lunch from 19€. AE, MC, V. Lunch & dinner daily. Métro: Louvre-Rivoli. Map p 102.*

★ Le Grand 8 MONTMARTRE

TRADITIONAL FRENCH Bohemian-bourgeois foodies climb up Montmartre's Butte for the natural wines (some of the best in town), wonderful views of the Sacré Coeur, and well-executed, wholesome dishes, such as duck with roasted apples and orange-blossom crème brûlée. Divine! *8 rue Lamarck, 18th. ☎ 01-42-55-04-55. Entrees 17€–22€. MC, V. Lunch & dinner Tues–Sun. Métro: Château Rouge or Anvers (then funiculaire de Montmartre). Map p 101.*

★★★ Le Grand Véfour

TUILERIES *TRADITIONAL FRENCH* This romantic, historic, expensive place is a favorite of food critics. Specialties include lamb cooked with sweet wine, Breton lobster, and cabbage sorbet in dark-chocolate sauce. *17 rue de Beaujolais, 1st. ☎ 01-42-96-56-27. www.grand-vefour.com. Reservations far in advance. Entrees 80€–110€, prix-fixe lunch 80€, prix-fixe dinner 240€. AE, DC, MC, V. Lunch & dinner*

An elegant table awaits discerning diners at Le Grand Véfour.

Mon–Thurs, lunch Fri. Closed Aug. Métro: Louvre-Palais Royal or Pyramides. Map p 102.

★ Le Potager du Marais

MARAIS *VEGETARIAN* Vegetarians flock to this organic offering, arguably the best vegetarian restaurant in Paris. Dishes are so tasty that meat eaters won't complain. The welcome is warm, and many items are gluten-free. 22 rue Rambuteau, 3rd. ☎ 01-57-40-98-57. Entrees 11€–20€. MC, V. Lunch & dinner daily. Métro: Rambuteau. Map p 102.

★★ Le Timbre LUXEMBOURG

FRENCH ["]The Stamp" is, as its name implies, a tiny restaurant. But what it lacks in space, it makes up for in the kitchen with such delicious dishes as asparagus and crumbled Parmesan, pork with red onions, and moelleux au chocolat (squishy chocolate cake). There's an appetizing wine list, too. *3 rue Ste-Beuve, 6th.* ☎ *01-45-49-10-40. www.restaurantletimbre.com. Lunch 27€, 3-course menu 42€. MC, V. Lunch & dinner Tues–Sat. Métro: Vavin. Map p 104.*

★ Les Fables de la Fontaine

EIFFEL TOWER *SEAFOOD* One of the city's best seafood

restaurants draws crowds with its fresh fried shrimp, baked sea bass with a rich, creamy sauce, big bowls of mussels, and fine oysters. The restaurant is small, so tables fill up quickly. Book the second sitting if you want to linger. *131 rue St-Dominique, 7th.* ☎ *01-44-18-37-55. www.lesfablesdelafontaine.net. Entrees 33€–40€, lunch menus from 30€. MC, V. Lunch & dinner Tues–Sat. Métro: Ecole Militaire. Map p 104.*

★ Les Petites Sorcières

DENFERT ROCHEREAU *NORTHERN FRENCH* TV chef Ghislaine Arabian offers specialties from Flanders in this off-the-beaten-path neo-bistro near Denfert Rochereau. Sip a full-bodied red and then tuck into such perfectly executed classics as *waterzooï* (cod in cream-and-vegetable sauce) and Brussels waffles with ice cream. One of the best value lunch menus in Paris. *12 rue Liancourt, 14th.* ☎ *01-43-21-95-68. Prix-fixe lunch 25€, entrees 25€–35€. MC, V. Lunch & dinner Tues–Sat. Métro: Mouton-Devernet or Denfert Rochereau. Map p 104.*

★★★ L'Hôtel Thoumieux

INVALIDES *BRASSERIE/CONTEMPORARY FRENCH* This is one of the most exciting places to eat in Paris. There's the Art Deco–inspired downstairs brasserie, **Le Thoumieux,** which serves such dishes as scallops and cheese macaroni, and hot churros in sticky chocolate sauce to well-heeled Parisians. Upstairs in **Chez Jean-François Piège,** the chef of the same name delights foodies with such dreamy dishes as asparagus latticed with black-truffle cream and coated in Cantal-cheese emulsion, or crayfish in an herb broth with foie gras. *In the Hôtel Thoumieux, 79 rue St-Dominique, 7th.* ☎ *01-47-05-79-00. www.thoumieux.fr. Reservations required. Brasserie prix-fixe lunch 29€, 3-course average 50€. Chez Jean-François*

Piège prix-fixe menus 119€–239€. AE, DC, MC, V. Lunch & dinner daily. Métro: La Tour-Maubourg. Map p 104.

★★ **Mon Vieil Ami** ÎLE ST-LOUIS *CONTEMPORARY FRENCH* This slice of gastronomy is where chef Antoine Westermann prepares traditional French cuisine with a modern twist. Vegetables take pride of place alongside perfect meat and fish, creating such wonderful *plats* as slow-braised roebuck with celery, quince, and chestnuts, and seafood casserole topped with tomatoes and tender baby squid. 65 rue St-Louis-en-l'Île, 4th. ☎ 01-40-46-01-35. www.mon-vieil-ami.com. Reservations required. Prix-fixe menu 38€–48€, entrees 15€–25€. AE, MC, V. Lunch & dinner Wed–Sun, dinner Tues. Métro: Pont Marie. Map p 102.

kids **Pink Flamingo** CANAL ST-MARTIN PIZZA Not only are the Pink's pizzas quirky (try the Poulidor, with goat cheese and sliced duck breast), they're also put together with the best, freshest ingredients, and the crusts are made with organic flour. If you picnic by the canal, take a pink helium balloon, find your spot, and wait for the pizza delivery boy to cycle to you. There are other locations at 105 rue Vieille du Temple, 3rd; 23 rue d'Aligre, 12th; and 30 rue Muller, 18th. 67 rue Bichat, 10th. ☎ 01-42-02-31-70. www.pinkflamingo pizza.com. Pizzas from 11€. MC, V. Lunch & dinner Tues–Sun. Métro: Jacques Bonsergent. Map p 102.

★ kids **Schwartz's** MARAIS *JEWISH* This New York–style Jewish deli bustles throughout the day with hungry folk looking to fill up on smoked herring, pastrami, chunky bagels, burgers, and hot dogs. The cheesecake is a treat, too. 16 rue des Ecouffes, 4th. ☎ 01-48-87-31-29. www.schwartzsdeli.fr. Entrees 9€–19€. AE, DC, MC, V. Lunch & dinner Mon–Sat, brunch Sun. Métro: St-Paul. Map p 102.

★★★ **Septime** NORTHEAST PARIS *CONTEMPORARY FRENCH* People cross the city for this rustic-chic eatery near Bastille. The reason? Such dishes as succulent pork with caramelized rutabaga, smoked duck with leek and ricotta, mackerel with asparagus, and roasted apple with cream—all flawless. The lunch menu is a steal at 28€. 80 rue de Charonne, 11th. ☎ 01-43-67-38-29. www.septime-charonne.fr. Entrees 25€, prix-fixe lunch 28€. MC, V. Lunch & dinner Tues–Fri, dinner Mon. Métro: Charonne. Map p 102.

★★★ **The Shangri-La Restaurants** CHAILLOT *FRENCH & ASIAN* The palatial **Hôtel Shangri-La** (p 101) gives you no fewer than three fabulous high-end eating opportunities: **Shang Palace,** the city's first-ever gourmet Cantonese restaurant; **L'Abeille,** a marvelous gastronomic French restaurant overlooking the interior garden; and in the hotel's epicenter (set beneath a 1930s Eiffel-style cupola), **La Bauhinia** brasserie, which serves lip-smacking Chinese and French dishes so that you can mix and match. 10 av. Iéna, 16th. ☎ 01-53-67-19-98. www.shangri-la. com. Entrees 60€–90€, prix-fixe lunch from 80€. AE, DC, MC, V. Lunch & dinner daily. Métro: Iéna. Map p 101.

★★★ **Taillevent** CHAMPS ELYSEES *MODERN FRENCH* Occupying a 19th-century town house off the Champs-Elysées with paneled rooms and crystal chandeliers, this is one of the city's best gastronomic restaurants. Try the sausage of Breton lobster, the watercress soup with sevruga caviar, or the salmon in sea salt. 15 rue Lamennais, 8th. ☎ 01-44-95-15-01. www.taillevent.com. Reservations 6 weeks in advance. Prix-fixe menu 75€–200€. AE, DC, MC, V. Lunch & dinner Mon–Fri. Closed Aug. Métro: George-V. Map p 101. ●

Nightlife Best Bets

Best **Bohemian Bar**
★ Chez Prune, *36 rue Beaurepaire, 10th* (p 122)

Best **Chic Cocktails**
★★★ Le Ballroom, *52 rue Jean-Jacques Rousseau, 1st* (p 123)

Best **Place to Steal a Kiss**
★★ La Palette, *43 rue de Seine, 6th* (p 123)

Best **Wine Bar**
★★ Le Baron Rouge, *1 rue Théophile-Roussel, 12th* (p 124)

Best **Nikka Bar outside Japan**
Curio Parlor, *16 rue des Bernardins* (p 122)

Best **for Students**
★ Académie de la Bière, *88 bd. de Port-Royal, 5th* (p 121)

Best **for Fans of Papa**
★★★ Harry's Bar, *5 rue Daunou, 2nd* (p 122)

Best **for Dinner & a Boogie**
★ Wanderlust, *32 quai d'Austerlitz, 13th* (p 120)

Best **Hip Hangout**
★★ Chez Jeanette, *47 rue du Faubourg St-Denis, 10th* (p 122)

Best **for Cocktails & Frites**
Dédé La Frite, *135 rue Montmartre, 2nd* (p 122)

Best **Waterfront Location**
★★ Batofar, *11 quai François Mauriac,13th* (p 120)

Best **Atypical Club**
★★ Le Dandy, *26 rue Pierre Fontaine, 9th* (p 120)

Best **for the Latest Electro Sounds**
★★ Rex Club, *5 bd. Poissonnière, 2nd* (p 120)

Best **Gay Bars**
Open Café & Café Cox, *15 & 17 rue des Archives, 4th* (p 121)

Best **Lesbian Bar**
La Champmeslé, *4 rue Chabanais, 2nd* (p 121)

Best **Boudoir**
★★★ Le Bar de L'Hôtel, *13 rue des Beaux-Arts, 6th* (p 123)

The cocktails served at Curio Parlor are hard to find outside Japan.

Previous page: Harry's, once frequented by Hemingway, still attracts a fun expat crowd.

Right Bank (8th & 16th–17th)

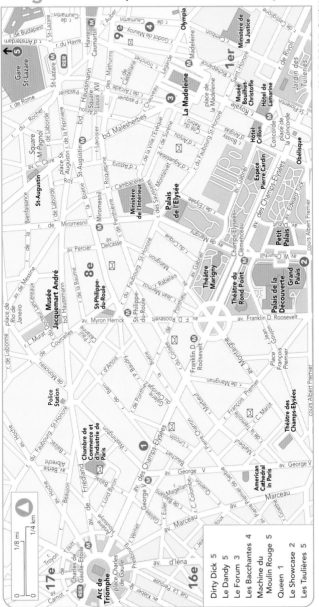

Dirty Dick 5
Le Dandy 5
Le Forum 3
Les Bacchantes 4
Machine du Moulin Rouge 5
Queen 1
Le Showcase 2
Les Taulières 5

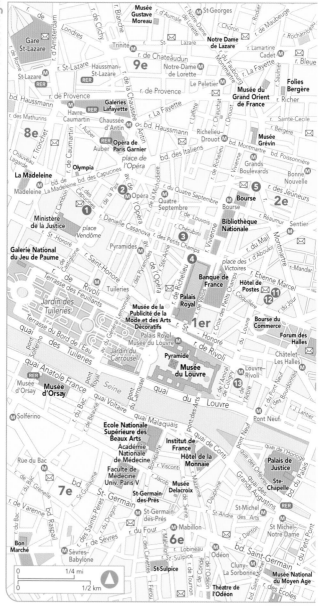

Chez Jeanette 7
Chez Prune 8
Dédé La Frite 5
Harry's Bar 2
Juveniles 4
La Belle Hortense 15
La Champmeslé 3
Le Ballroom 12
Le Baron Rouge 16
Le Calbar 16
Le Fumoir 13
Le Tango 10
Nouveau Casino 9
Ô Château 11
Open Café &
 Café Cox 14
Pozada 16
Rex Club 6
Wine by One 1

Left Bank (5th–6th)

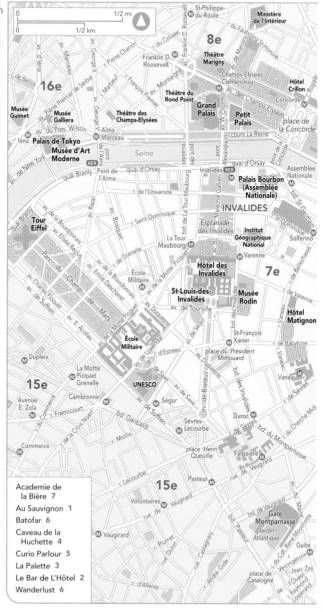

Académie de la Bière 7
Au Sauvignon 1
Batofar 6
Caveau de la Huchette 4
Curio Parlour 5
La Palette 3
Le Bar de L'Hôtel 2
Wanderlust 6

Nightlife A to Z

Dance Clubs

★★ **Batofar** BIBLIOTHEQUE
At this hip club, on a converted barge on the Seine, the rotating DJs attract hundreds of 20- and 30-somethings. In the summer, the quayside turns into an extension of the boat, with food, a bar, and deck chairs. *11 quai François Mauriac, 13th. ☎ 09-71-25-50-61. www.bato-far.org. Cover free–15€. Métro: Quai de la Gare. Map p 118.*

Caveau de la Huchette LATIN QUARTER   This rocking club has an emphasis on good times and loud funk, jazz, and classic rock; the crowd tends to be in their 30s and above. *5 rue de la Huchette, 5th. ☎ 01-43-26-65-05. www.caveaudela-huchette.fr. Cover 10€–14€. Métro: St-Michel. Map p 118.*

Le Dandy MONTMARTRE/ PIGALLE   This funky club is dressed up like a Parisian apartment, with a red boudoir/bar and a pastel shaded-bedroom kitted out with a piano and a bed. Music is predominantly deep house and nu disco. Live bands occasionally pump things up on weekends. *26 rue Pierre Fontaine, 9th. ☎ 01-40-29-19-85. www.dandyclub.fr. Cover free–25€. Métro: Pigalle. Map p 115.*

Le Showcase CHAMPS ELYSEES Underneath pont Alexandre III, inside an old boat hangar, this happening club packs in the young and energetic for nightly shows by French and international rock, pop, and electro bands. There are DJ nights with renowned names, too. *Pont Alexandre III, 8th. ☎ 01-45-61-25-43. www.showcase.fr. Cover up to 20€. Métro: Champs-Elysées Clémenceau. Map p 115.*

★★ **Machine du Moulin Rouge** MONTMARTRE   In the nightclub adjoining Paris's most famous cabaret, this is the latest hot spot for electronic music lovers. Expect DJ sets by famous names, a big dance floor, and youthful fauna soaking up the vibes. *90 bd. de Clichy, 18th. ☎ 01-53-41-88-89. www.lamachine dumoulinrouge.com. Cover free–30€. Métro: Blanche. Map p 115.*

★★ **Nouveau Casino** OBERKAMPF   This is one of the city's hottest clubs from Wednesday to Saturday. From club to techno with stop-offs at electro and rock, it's a good place to see how the French get down. *109 rue Oberkampf, 11th. ☎ 01-43-57-57-40. www.nouveaucasino.net. Cover free–20€. Métro: Parmentier. Map p 116.*

Queen CHAMPS ELYSEES   This very-late-night, gay-friendly club attracts a mixed crowd of corporate workers kicking back, ladies out for a night of dancing, and tourists in the know. Occasionally attracts international DJs. *102 av. des Champs-Elysées, 8th. ☎ 01-53-89-08-90. www.queen.fr. Cover free–20€. Métro: George-V. Map p 115.*

★★ **Rex Club** GRANDS BOULEVARDS   This place is known for its cutting-edge electronic music, with top DJs playing weekly and frequent free nights. Check local listings to see who's at the helm. *5 bd. Poissonnière, 2nd. ☎ 01-42-36-10-96. www.rexclub.com. Cover up to 20€. Métro: Bonne Nouvelle. Map p 116.*

★★ **Wanderlust** AUSTERLITZ Start the night in the restaurant (where different chefs take the helm every 4 months), then cross the deck to the club, where stylish crowds gyrate. Dress up if you want to get in—this is the trendiest place in Paris right now. *32 quai d'Austerlitz, 13th. ☎ 01-70-74-41-74*

Nightlife Basics

Low-key bars (and even cafes) are a big part of Paris nightlife, open from 7am to 1am or 2am. Cranking things up a notch are trendy cocktail joints and night bars that usually open at 6pm and close at 5am.

If you're interested in getting into the capital's trendiest night-clubs, you should know that Parisian bouncers are extremely picky. Dress up, smile, and hope they let you in; or ensure entry the expensive way by reserving a table with bottle service, where you pay around 150€ for a bottle of champagne or a spirit. If you don't buy a table, club entry usually costs around 30€ and may include one free drink at the bar.

The legal drinking age in France is 18. Expect to pay around 5€ for a glass of wine or 4€ for beer in a bar or cafe and 13€ to 20€ for a cocktail. Drinks in nightclubs usually start at 10€.

(restaurant; no phone in club). http://wanderlustparis.com. No cover. Métro/RER: Gare d'Austerlitz. Map p 118.

Gay & Lesbian Bars & Clubs

La Champmeslé BOURSE Dim lighting, background music, and banquettes set the scene at this cozy meeting place for lesbians and gays in a 300-year-old building. There's fortune-telling every Tuesday night and art exhibits every month. *4 rue Chabanais, 2nd.* ☎ *01-42-96-85-20. www.lachampmesle.com. Métro: Pyramides or Bourse. Map p 116.*

Le Tango (aka La Boîte à Frissons) REPUBLIQUE This wacky hetero-friendly gay and lesbian dance hall plays cheesy Madonna songs and accordion music alike. Couples practice dancing the fox-trot and tango early on, and then a DJ takes over and plays everything except techno. *13 rue au Maire, 2nd.* ☎ *01-42-72-17-78. www.boite-a-frissons.fr. Cover 8€ (free on Thurs). Métro: Arts et Métiers. Map p 116.*

Les Taulières MONTMARTRE Away from the Marais crowds, this

lesbian and gay bar is an ode to kitsch, with furry chairs, vintage barstools, and comic strips on the walls. DJs spice the night away with cool electro sounds on week-ends. *10 rue de la Fontain du But.* ☎ *01-42-58-60-64. No cover. Métro: Lamarck-Caulincourt. Map p 115.*

Open Café & Café Cox MARAIS This pair of gay men's bars includes two independent businesses, but there's so much traffic between them that they're often thought of as a single place. You'll find the most mixed gay crowd in Paris here. *15 & 17 rue des Archives, 4th. Open Café:* ☎ *01-42-72-26-18. www.opencafe.fr. Café Cox:* ☎ *01-42-72-08-00. www.cox.fr. Métro: Hôtel-de-Ville. Map p 115.*

Pubs & Bars

★ **Académie de la Bière** LATIN QUARTER This rustic-looking "academy of beer" can get down-right raucous. Most of the beers on tap come from Belgium. Soak it up with delicious *moules-frites*. *88 bd. de Port-Royal, 5th.* ☎ *01-43-54-66-65. www.academie-biere.com. RER: Port Royal. Map p 118.*

The decor of Chez Jeanette, in the 10th arrondissement, is vintage 1940s.

★★ **Dirty Dick** PIGALLE   This hip new cocktail joint, decorated in tiki memorabilia, takes you back to 1960s Hawaii. Choose between 55 types of rum and more than 20 different cocktails, including—if you dare—the *Mula Mexicana*, a fiery mix of tequila, mint, ginger, and chili pepper! *10 rue Frochot, 9th.* ☎ *01-48-78-74-58. Métro: Pigalle. Map p 115.*

Chez Jeanette STRASBOURG-SAINT-DENIS   The decor in this bar has changed little since the 1940s. Nowadays crowds of trendy 30-somethings lap up the cheap wine, while the occasional old regular sweeps in, Jack Russell in tow, oblivious to the change of clientele. *47 rue du Faubourg St-Denis, 10th.* ☎ *01-47-70-30-89. Métro: Strasbourg-St-Denis or Château Eau. Map p 116.*

★ **Chez Prune** CANAL SAINT-MARTIN   This bobo magnet serves excellent, well-priced food, including some vegetarian dishes (from 13€), coffee, beer, and wine to local arty types and cool do-littlers taking in the canal-side view. *36 rue Beaurepaire, 10th.* ☎ *01-42-41-30-47. Métro: République. Map p 116.*

Curio Parlor SAINT-GERMAIN-DES-PRES   This bar specializes in Nikka Japanese whisky, one of only a few such establishments outside the Land of the Rising Sun. Tequila and whisky cocktails are also well made here, as are a myriad of other concoctions you won't find anywhere else in town. *16 rue des Bernardins, 5th.* ☎ *01-47-07-12-47. Métro: St-Germain-des-Prés. Map p 118.*

Dédé La Frite BOURSE   Near the stock exchange, Dédé serves beers and cocktails to after-work crowds. Just when you fancy a nibble, the wafting aroma of fries and burgers hits your nose, and then later on, the music is cranked up. *135 rue Montmartre, 2nd.* ☎ *01-40-41-99-90. Métro: Bourse. Map p 116.*

★★★ **Harry's Bar** OPERA   This place is sacred to Hemingway disciples as the place where he and the rest of the ambulance corps drank themselves silly during the Spanish Civil War. This bar is responsible for the White Lady and the Sidecar, along with numerous damaged livers. A pianist plays in the cellar; the area upstairs is somewhat less sophisticated. Filled with expats, this place is more fun than you might think. *5 rue Daunou, 2nd.* ☎ *01-42-61-71-14. www.harrys-bar.fr. Métro: Opéra or Pyramides. Map p 116.*

★★ **Le Calbar** NORTHEAST PARIS   Oh la la! The gimmick at this trendy bar near Bastille is the barmen's garb: boxer shorts (*calbar* is French slang for underwear). But there's nothing risqué here—just fantabulous cocktails prepared with whisky, vodka, champagne, or rum.

82 rue de Charenton, 12th. ☎ 01-84-06-18-90. http://lecalbarcocktail.com. Métro. Ledru Rollin or Bastille. Map p 116.

★ **La Palette** ST-GERMAIN-DES-PRES   This is a favorite rendezvous for students from the nearby fine-arts school. It's also rather romantic (especially the fresco-painted back room). A drink here means following in the steps of Ernest Hemingway and Jim Morrison. A handy base for exploring Saint-Germain's art galleries. 43 rue de Seine, 6th. ☎ 01-43-26-68-15. Métro: Odéon. Map p 118.

★★ **Le Ballroom** PALAIS-ROYAL/ LES HALLES   After a juicy steak in the upstairs Beef Club, descend the "secret" staircase to one of the city's best underground cocktail bars. It feels as though you've stepped into a speakeasy, with dark lighting and vintage decor (not to mention the Mafia-like bouncers). Expect well-mixed drinks. 52 rue Jean-Jacques Rousseau, 1st. ☎ 09-52-52-89-34. www.eccbeefclub.com. Métro: Louvre-Rivoli or Les Halles. Map p 116.

★★★ **Le Bar de L'Hôtel** ST-GERMAIN-DES-PRES   This hotel bar is appropriately theatrical (a Victorian color scheme, baroque touches) when you consider that its regulars tend to be in the film industry—or want to be. This was the hotel where Oscar Wilde died, impoverished and alone; it's a lovely historic place for a drink and a ponder. 13 rue des Beaux-Arts, 6th. ☎ 01-44-41-99-00. www.l-hotel.com. Métro: St-Germain-des-Prés. Map p 118.

★ **Le Forum** MADELEINE   This smart, business-crowd favorite is like a London private club—all oak paneling, single malts, and brass. On the drinks menu (aside from the digestifs) are delicious cocktails, such as the Pornstar Martini (vodka, passion fruit, and vanilla liquor). 4 bd. Malesherbes, 8th. ☎ 01-42-65-37-86. www.bar-le-forum.com. Métro: Madeleine. Map p 115.

★★ **Le Fumoir** LOUVRE   An intriguing mix of hip Parisians and Euro-loungers comes to linger over wine, cocktails, or good food in a book-lined setting that recalls the cafes of French Indochina in the 1930s. 6 rue de l'Amiral de Coligny, 1st. ☎ 01-42-92-00-24. www.lefumoir.com. Métro: Louvre-Rivoli. Map p 116.

Wine Bars

★ **Au Sauvignon** ST-GERMAIN-DES-PRES   This tiny bar has tables overflowing onto the terrace, where a cheerful crowd downs wines from the cheapest Beaujolais to the priciest Grand Cru. 80 rue des St-Pères, 7th. ☎ 01-45-48-49-02. Métro: Sèvres-Babylone. Map p 118.

With its frescoes in the back room, La Palette is a magnet for art students.

Rich conversations blossom within the book-lined walls of La Belle Hortense in the Marais.

★ **Juveniles** BOURSE This sleek place with a trendy crowd prides itself on its enormous wine cellar with labels from around the world. *47 rue de Richelieu, 1st.* ☎ *01-42-97-46-49. Métro: Palais Royal. Map p 116.*

La Belle Hortense MARAIS The fact that this quirky bar has a bookshop within its walls makes it a perpetual favorite for bookish wine lovers. *31 vieille du Temple, 4th.* ☎ *01-48-04-71-60. www.cafeine.com. Métro: Hôtel-de-Ville. Map p 116.*

★★ **Le Baron Rouge** BASTILLE Be prepared to fight for elbow room at this popular locals' haunt (opposite the Aligre market), where excellent wine is sold by the glass and drunk on wine barrels posing as tables. Grab a plate of charcuterie or oysters (when in season). *1 rue Théophile-Roussel, 12th.* ☎ *01-42-72-76-85. Métro: St-Paul. Map p 116.*

★★ **Les Bacchantes** MADELEINE This place just down the road from Printemps department store is a top spot for a post-shopping tipple. Around 50 wines grace the board, so be prepared for indecision. Tiles and exposed beams add character. *21 rue Caumartin, 9th.* ☎ *01-42-65-25-35. www.lesbacchantes.fr. Métro: Opéra or Madeleine. Map p 115.*

★ **Ô Château** LOUVRE A quality wine list, screens for rugby matches, tasting lessons, *Vinomatic* wine dispensers that let you decide how much you taste, and good food platters make this a huge draw for oenophiles. *68 rue Jean-Jaques Rousseau, 1st.* ☎ *01-44-73-97-80. www.o-chateau.fr. Métro: Louvre-Rivoli. Map p 116.*

★★ **Pozada** NORTHEAST PARIS/NATION Off the beaten tourist track in trendifying Nation, this place is about two things: first-rate wine for every budget and delicious contemporary French cuisine. Friendly staff, a tasting area and shop, and regular concerts top off the experience. *2 rue Guénot, 11th.* ☎ *01-43-70-63-24. www.pozada.fr. Métro: Nation. Map p 116.*

★★ **Wine by One** MADELEINE After-work crowds pile into this playful futuristic bar, where touchscreen pads link to computerized wine-tasting distributors containing more than 100 different bottles. Pair the vintages with platters of cheese and charcuterie from 12€ and learn about the wines you're tasting from the gracious staff. *9 rue des Capucines, 1st.* ☎ *01-42-60-85-76, www.winebyone.com. Métro: Madeleine or Tuileries. Map p 116.* ●

Arts & Entertainment Best Bets

Best **Theater for Musicals**
★★★ Théâtre du Châtelet,
1 place du Châtelet, 1st (p 136)

Best **Place to Walk in the Phantom's Footsteps**
★★★ Opéra Garnier,
Place de l'Opéra, 9th (p 135)

Best **Place to Hear Classical Music**
La Salle Pleyel, *252 rue du Faubourg St-Honoré, 8th (p 134)*

Best **Theater**
★ Comédie Française, *Place Colette, 1st (p 135)*

Best **Drag Show**
Cabaret Michou, *80 rue des Martyrs, 18th (p 131)*

Best **Place to hear Modern French Chanson**
★ Les Trois Baudets, *64 bd. de Clichy, 18th (p 133)*

Best **Place to See the Cancan**
★ Moulin Rouge, *Place Blanche, 18th (p 131)*

Best **Chic Cabaret**
★★ Le Lido de Paris, *116 bis av. des Champs-Elysées, 8th (p 131)*

Best **Place for 20-Somethings**
★ La Flèche d'Or, *102 bis rue de Bagnolet, 20th (p 132)*

Best **Place to See & Be Seen**
★ New Morning, *7–9 rue des Petites-Ecuries, 10th (p 134)*

Best **Overall Jazz Club**
★★★ Au Duc des Lombards,
42 rue des Lombards, 1st (p 132)

Best **Nouvelle Orleans Jazz**
★★★ Le Sunset/Le Sunside,
60 rue des Lombards, 1st (p 133)

Best **Live Music with your meal**
★ La Bellevilloise, *19–21 rue Boyer, 20th (p 132)*

Best **Indie Rock Concerts**
La Boule Noire, *120 bd. de Rochechouart,18th (p 132)*

Previous page: The Grand Staircase and rococo interior of the Opéra Garnier.
Below: The Opéra Bastille was inaugurated in 1989 for the Revolution's bicentennial.

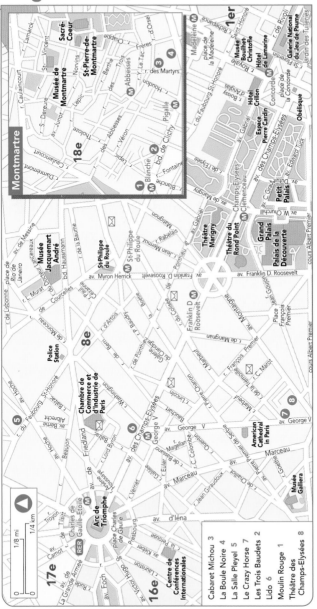

Right Bank (8th & 18th)

Right Bank (1st–4th & 9th–11th)

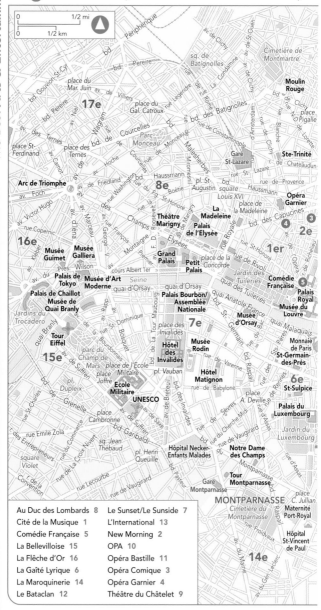

Au Duc des Lombards 8
Cité de la Musique 1
Comédie Française 5
La Bellevilloise 15
La Flèche d'Or 16
La Gaîté Lyrique 6
La Maroquinerie 14
Le Bataclan 12

Le Sunset/Le Sunside 7
L'International 13
New Morning 2
OPA 10
Opéra Bastille 11
Opéra Comique 3
Opéra Garnier 4
Théâtre du Châtelet 9

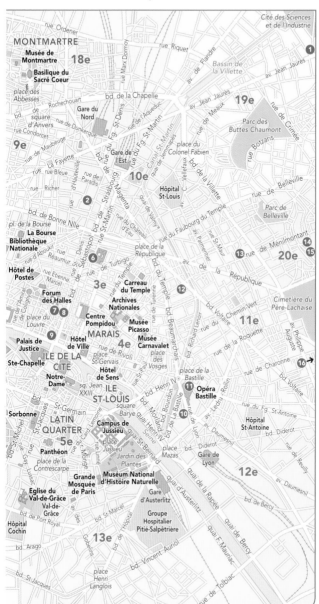

Cité des Sciences et de l'Industrie

rue Ordener

MONTMARTRE

Musée de Montmartre

18e

rue Riquet

Basilique du Sacré Coeur

place des Abbesses

av. de Flandre

Bassin de la Villette

av. Jean Jaurès

❶

rue de Rochechouart

Gare du Nord

bd. de la Chapelle

av. Jean Jaurès

19e

av. de Meaux

rue de Crimée

rue Bolzaris

square d'Anvers

rue de Dunkerque

rue du Fg. St-Denis

rue de l'Aqueduc

rue du Fg. St-Martin

place du Colonel Fabien

Parc des Buttes Chaumont

rue Condorcet

9e

rue de Maubeuge

La Fayette

rue Bleue

rue d'Hauteville

rue de Paradis

Gare de l'Est

rue du Fg. St-Martin

Canal St-Martin

bd. de la Villette

rue de Belleville

rue Richer

bd. de Strasbourg

10e

quai de Valmy

Hôpital St-Louis

rue de Belleville

Parc de Belleville

bd. de Bonne Nlle

pl. de la Bourse

La Bourse

Bibliothèque Nationale

rue Réaumur

bd. de Sébastopol

rue du Château d'Eau

rue du Faubourg du Temple

av. Parmentier

rue St-Maur

rue de Ménilmontant

❶❹

Hôtel de Postes

rue d'Aboukir

rue St-Denis

rue de Turbigo

place de la République

bd. du Temple

av.

de

la

République

20e

❶❺

rue Etienne Marcel

❻

3e

Carreau du Temple

❶❷

rue de Turenne

bd. Voltaire

bd. Richard Lenoir

rue du Chemin-Vert

11e

Cimetière du Père-Lachaise

Forum des Halles

❼❽

Archives Nationales

Centre Pompidou

MARAIS

Musée Picasso

Musée Carnavalet

rue de la Roquette

av. Philippe Auguste

Palais de Justice

❾

Hôtel de Ville

4e

rue de Rivoli

place des Vosges

place de la Bastille

av. Ledru-Rollin

rue de Charonne

❶❻➔

bd. Voltaire

Ste-Chapelle

ÎLE DE LA CITÉ

Hôtel de Sens

rue St-Paul

place St-Gervais

bd. Henri IV

❶❶

Opéra Bastille

rue du Fg. St-Antoine

Notre-Dame

sq. Jean XXIII

ÎLE ST-LOUIS

square Barye

bd. Morland

❶❶

quai Henri IV

rue de Lyon

Hôpital St-Antoine

bd. Diderot

Sorbonne

St-Germain

LATIN QUARTER

rue du Card Lemoine

Campus de Jussieu

quai St-Bernard

place Mazas

av. Daumesnil

Gare de Lyon

rue de Reuilly

Panthéon

5e

place Jussieu

Jardin des Plantes

bd.

Diderot

12e

av. Daumesnil

place de la Contrescarpe

Grande Mosquée de Paris

Muséum National d'Histoire Naturelle

Gare d'Austerlitz

quai d'Austerlitz

quai de la Rapée

bd. de Bercy

Église du Val-de-Grâce

Val-de-Grâce

Groupe Hospitalier Pitié-Salpêtrière

quai F. Mauriac

Hôpital Cochin

bd. de Port Royal

13e

bd. St-Marcel

bd. de l'Hôpital

bd. Arago

bd. St-Jacques

place Henri Langlois

bd. Vincent Auriol

rue de Tolbiac

Left Bank (5th–6th)

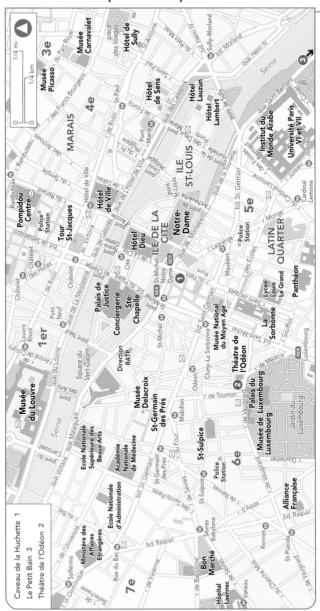

Caveau de la Huchette 1
Le Petit Bain 3
Théâtre de l'Odéon 2

Arts & Entertainment A to Z

The windmill atop the Moulin Rouge is a landmark in Montmartre.

Cabarets

Cabaret Michou PIGALLE This eccentric place is run by a veteran impresario whose 20 cross-dressing belles lip-sync to Whitney Houston and Mireille Mathieu while wearing bizarre costumes. If you don't have dinner, you must stand at the bar and pay a compulsory 40€ for your first drink. *80 rue des Martyrs, 18th.* ☎ *01-46-06-16-04. www.michou. com. Cover including dinner (not drinks) & show 110€– 140€. Métro: Pigalle. Map p 127.*

★ **Le Crazy Horse** CHAMPS ELYSEES This sophisticated joint's nude revue thrives on genuinely good choreography and the beauty of the girls, who dance dressed in little more than light. Not surprisingly, it's popular with businessmen, but women too will be surprised at how mesmerizing the show is. *12 av. George-V, 8th.* ☎ *01-47-23-32-32. www.lecrazy horseparis.com. Reservations*

recommended. *Cover including 2 drinks per person 125€, show only 105€. Dining options available. Métro: George-V or Alma-Marceau. Map p 127.*

★★ **Le Lido** CHAMPS ELYSEES This glossy club puts on multimillion-euro performances in a dramatic reworking of the classic Parisian cabaret show, with special effects, including aerial and aquatic ballets—even an occasional ice rink. *116 bis av. des Champs-Elysées, 8th.* ☎ *01-40-76-56-10. www.lido.fr. Show only 90€, show w/ half bottle champagne per person 105€, dinner & show 160€–300€. Métro: George-V. Map p 127.*

★ **Moulin Rouge** MONTMARTRE Toulouse-Lautrec immortalized this windmill-topped building and its scantily clad cancan dancers (this is where the risqué dance was invented). Today, it's true to its original theme and very cheesy, but the dancing is perfectly synchronized, and the girls are all beautiful. *Place Blanche, 18th.* ☎ *01-53-09-82-82. www.moulinrouge.fr. Show only 99€, show & half bottle champagne 109€, dinner & show 180€–210€. Métro: Blanche. Map p 127.*

Jazz, Rock & More
★★★ Au Duc des Lombards
CHATELET   This thriving jazz club has seen all the greats of Paris's jazz era pass through its doors. Today, it features performances nightly that range in style from free jazz to hard bop. Tables can be reserved, and meals (prepared with mostly fair-trade produce) are served. *42 rue des Lombards, 1st.* ☎ *01-42-33-22-88. www.ducdeslombards.com. Cover varies. Métro: Châtelet. Map p 128.*

★ Caveau de la Huchette
LATIN QUARTER   This celebrated jazz cave draws a young crowd, mostly university students, who dance to the music of well-known jazz combos. Robespierre hung out here in his time, so you can tell everyone you're here for the history. *5 rue de la Huchette, 5th.* ☎ *01-43-26-65-05. www.caveaudelahuchette.fr. Cover 10€–14€. Métro: St-Michel. RER: St-Michel-Notre-Dame. Map p 130.*

★★ La Bellevilloise
MENILMON-TANT   This multidisciplinary venue (set inside France's first cooperative building) has several bars, two restaurants, a nightclub, an exhibition space, and a concert hall where some of Paris's most exciting bands have been launched. It's a place to relax, soak up the atmosphere, and spend the whole evening. *19–21 rue Boyer, 20th.* ☎ *01-46-36-07-07. www.labellevilloise.com. Cover varies. Metro: Gambetta, or Ménilmontant. Map p 128.*

La Boule Noire
PIGALLE   The Black Ball is one of those intimate, divey Parisian haunts that attract such biggies as the Dandy Warhols, Metallica, Cat Power, Franz Ferdinand, and Jamie Cullum. Despite the star-studded lineup, the cover tends to hover around the 20€ mark, making this one of the cheapest venues around. *120 bd. Rochechouart, 75018.* ☎ *01-49-25-81-75. www.laboule-noire.fr. Cover varies. Metro: Anvers or Pigalle. Map p 127.*

★★★ La Flèche d'Or
PERE LACHAISE   This funky rock, indie, and electro venue not only has highly credible acts (from both France and abroad), it has the

Indie bands are the staple fare at La Flèche d'Or, in the 20th arrondissement.

La Bellevilloise is an entertainment emporium housing multiple venues.

advantage of being set in a unique building—a former train station with a room that hangs over the tracks. This is a popular choice for trendy music buffs. *102 bis rue de Bagnolet, 20th.* ☎ *01-44-64-01-02. www.flechedor.fr. Cover varies. Métro: Alexandre-Dumas. Map p 128.*

★★ **La Gaité Lyrique** HAUT MARAIS   For those into digital art and off-beat culture, this former opera house (where Offenbach created the operetta genre) is a showcase for emerging digital art forms. After visiting the art installations, you can frequently attend an electronic pop/rock concert in the Grand Salle, whose walls are giant speakers. *3 bis rue Papin, 3rd.* ☎ *01-53-01-52-00. www.gaite-lyrique.net. Cover varies. Métro: Réamur-Sébastopol. Map p 128.*

Le Bataclan REPUBLIQUE Behind the brightly colored facade of this former music hall (established in 1864), the Bataclan is a flagship of Paris's music scene with top funk, rock, jazz, and hip-hop acts from across the globe. *50 bd. Voltaire, 11th.* ☎ *01-43-14-00-30. www.le-bataclan.com. Cover varies. Métro: Oberkampf. Map p 128.*

★ **Le Petit Bain** BIBLIOTHEQUE This wooden and chartreuse rectangle, floating on the Seine, is one of the city's best concert venues, with a stream of up-and-coming bands and a handful of well-known musicians. Dine in the restaurant beforehand or sip a cool *bière* on the upper terrace. Then watch Paris's lights reflect like diamonds on the water. *7 port de la Gare, 13th.* ☎ *01-80-48-49-81. www.petitbain. org. Cover varies. Métro: Quai de la Gare. Map p 130.*

Le Sunset/Le Sunside CHÂTELET This staple of the Parisian jazz circuit is two bars in one, with separate jazz shows going on simultaneously. The look is minimalist, and artists are both European and U.S.-based. Le Sunside favors classic jazz, and Le Sunset goes for electric jazz and world music. Take your pick. *60 rue des Lombards, 1st.* ☎ *01-40-26-46-60. www.sunset-sunside.com. Cover varies. Métro: Châtelet. Map p 128.*

Les Trois Baudets PIGALLE Between 1947 and 1966, this small theater launched more musical careers than anywhere else (Gainsbourg, Brel, and Henri Salvador all started here). Nowadays it's Paris's main francophone music theater, with a jam-packed program of rock, electro, folk, *chanson*, and slam poetry. *64 bd. de Clichy, 18th.* ☎ *01-42-62-33-33. www.lestrois baudets.com. Cover varies. Metro: Pigalle. Map p 127.*

L'International OBERKAMPF
Arty types flock to this grungy bar for its winning formula of cheap beer and free live music. A stream of on-the-up bands play here, making it a great joint in which to spot the talent of the future and get familiar with Paris's electro-rock scene. *5–7 rue Moret, 11th.* ☎ *01-49-29-76-45. www.linternational.fr. No cover. Métro: Menilmontant. Map p 128.*

Maroquinerie BELLEVILLE Up-and-coming rock acts take center stage at this hip concert venue, which doubles as a restaurant, bar, and literary cafe. You can easily spend the whole night here. *23 rue Boyer, 20th.* ☎ *01-40-33-35-05. www.lamaroquinerie.fr. Cover varies. Métro: Ménilmontant or Gambetta. Map p 128.*

★ **New Morning** EASTERN PARIS
Jazz fanatics pack this respected club to drink, talk, and dance, not to mention check each other out—this is one of the city's "it" places to see and be seen. Such celebs as Spike Lee and Prince have been spotted here. The club is popular with African and European musicians. *7–9 rue des Petites-Ecuries, 10th.* ☎ *01-45-23-51-41. www.new morning.com. Cover varies. Métro: Château d'Eau. Map p 128.*

OPA BASTILLE Join the young pretty things at industrial-chic OPA, which mixes live music with DJ nights (until 6am on weekends). Music-wise, expect a large dose of rock, pop, and electro. *9 rue Biscornet,*

12th. ☎ *01-46-28-12-90. www.opa-paris.com. Metro: Bastille. Map p 128.*

Opera, Dance & Classical
★ **Cité de la Musique** VILLETTE
This multimillion-euro structure incorporates a network of concert halls, libraries, and a museum on musical instruments across the ages. It hosts a variety of concerts from Renaissance music to modern works. *221 av. Jean Jaurès, 19th.* ☎ *01-44-84-44-84. www.cite-musique.fr. Tickets 8€–45€. Métro: Porte de Pantin. Map p 128.*

★★★ **La Salle Pleyel** TERNES
Some say this modern, wooden concert hall has the best acoustics in Paris. It also has an eclectic program, ranging from Baroque quartets to symphonic orchestras, opera recitals, and jazz ensembles—all usually big names. The cheapest tickets are for the rows behind the orchestra, but your enjoyment won't be impeded. *252 rue du Faubourg St-Honoré, 8th.* ☎ *01-42-56-13-13. www.sallepleyel.fr. Tickets 30€–190€. Métro: Ternes. Map p 127.*

★★★ **Opéra Bastille** BASTILLE
This huge contemporary building hosts outstanding opera performances, such as Mozart's *Marriage of Figaro* and Tchaikovsky's *Queen of Spades*, in its three concert halls. Symphony and dance performances are held here occasionally as well. *2 place de la Bastille, 4th.* ☎ *08-92-89-90-90. www.operadeparis.fr. Tickets for opera 5€–120€, dance 20€–80€. Métro: Bastille. Map p 128.*

★★ **Opéra Comique** BOURSE
Come to this charming venue, built in the 1880s, for light opera on a smaller scale than at the city's major opera houses. It's a lovely place to see *Carmen*, *Don Giovanni*, or *Tosca*. *5 rue Favart, 2nd.* ☎ *08-25-01-01-23.*

Best Free Shows in Paris

As you stroll along the river, keep your eyes peeled for free entertainment by street performers. In the summer months, the area at the southeastern tip of the Île de la Cité, behind Notre-Dame, becomes a stage of sorts when performance artists, musicians, jugglers, mimes, or magicians put on a show against the backdrop of the cathedral. The atmosphere is euphoric, the performances can be brilliant, and it makes for wonderful memories.

A later option is a walk along the Seine after 10pm. From the pont de Sully, take a pathway down on the Left Bank (away from Notre-Dame) to the Square Tino Rossi—a free open-air sculpture museum. You'll pass musicians and other performers, and when the music is good, spontaneous tango parties often break out at the water's edge.

www.opera-comique.com. Tickets 15€–100€. Métro: Richelieu-Drouot. Map p 128.

Theater Tip

Many theaters are closed over the summer, so check beforehand to avoid disappointment. Also, where possible make advance reservations: Parisians are enthusiastic theatergoers, and tickets can go like hotcakes.

★★★ Opéra Garnier OPERA

The Phantom did his fictional haunting here. Now the opera house is home to the city's ballet scene, although it still hosts opera from time to time. Charles Garnier's 1875 building is a rococo wonder with a centerpiece painted by Chagall. There are even beehives on the roof, which produce the Opéra honey for sale in the shop. *Place de l'Opéra, 9th.* ☎ 08-92-89-90-90. *www.operadeparis.fr. Tickets for dance 10€–70€, opera 20€–120€. Métro: Opéra. Map p 128.*

Théâtre des Champs-Elysées

CHAMPS ELYSEES National and international orchestras (such as the Vienna Philharmonic) fill this Art Deco theater with sound, to the delight of its well-dressed audiences. *15 av. Montaigne, 8th.* ☎ 01-49-52-50-50. *www.theatre champselysees.fr. Tickets 10€–115€. Métro: Alma–Marceau. Map p 127.*

Theater & Musicals

★ **Comédie Française** PALAIS ROYAL Those with even a modest understanding of French will enjoy a sparkling production at this national theater, where the main goal is to keep the classics alive while promoting contemporary authors. *Place Colette, 1st.* ☎ 08-25-10-16-80. *www.comedie-francaise.fr. Tickets 8€–60€. Métro: Palais Royal–Musée du Louvre. Map p 128.*

★ **Théâtre de l'Odéon** ODEON More than just a theater, the Odéon hosts debates on literature, philosophy, and European politics—a Euro enthusiasm that is translated on stage with quality plays in

Buying Tickets

The easiest way to get tickets nowadays is online, in advance, from the venue's website. If you're staying in a first-class hotel, your concierge can probably arrange your tickets, too. A service fee is added, but you won't waste precious sightseeing hours securing hard-to-get tickets.

Cheaper tickets, with discounts of up to 50 percent, can be found at the **Kiosque Théâtre,** 15 place de la Madeleine, 8th (no phone; Métro: Madeleine). It offers leftover tickets at about half-price on performance day. Tickets are sold Tuesday to Saturday from 12:30 to 8pm and Sunday from 2 to 8pm. Students with ID can often get last-minute tickets by inquiring at the box office an hour before curtain time.

If you haven't left for Paris yet and are having trouble getting advance tickets for cabaret performances, check with **Keith Prowse** (www.keithprowse.com). The company will mail tickets to you or leave tickets at the box office for pickup prior to the performance. There's a markup of about 25 percent over box-office prices on each ticket, which includes handling charges. Keith Prowse sells to customers all over the world, including the U.S., Canada, the U.K., Australia, and New Zealand. Another good place to try is any branch of the **FNAC** media store (or www.fnac.com). It handles tickets for most museums, concerts, and shows across France. The Champs Elysées branch is open until midnight (p 88).

---

different European languages, including English. *Place de l'Odéon, 6th.* ☎ *01-44-85-40-40. www. theatre-odeon.fr. Tickets 10€–40€. Métro: Odéon. Map p 130.*

★★★ Théâtre du Châtelet

CHÂTELET   This Belle Epoque masterpiece is the only place in Paris to perform Broadway standard musicals in English with full orchestras and parts sung by some of the world's best artists. Previous triumphs have included *Sweeney Todd* and *The Sound of Music.* The program is completed with top-notch classical concerts, opera, and dance. *1 place du Châtelet, 1st.* ☎ *01-40-28-28-28. www.chatelet-theatre.com. Tickets 20€–110€. Métro/RER: Châtelet. Map p 128.* ●

Lodging Best Bets

Best **Balcony Views**
Hôtel Edouard VII $$
39 av. de l'Opera, 2nd (p 147)

Best **for Romantics**
★ Hôtel Duc de St-Simon $$$
14 rue de St-Simon, 7th (p 146)

Best **Fun Design**
Five Hotel $$ *3 rue Flatters, 5th (p 144)*

Best **Boutique Hotel**
★ L'Hôtel $$$$ *13 rue des Beaux-Arts, 6th (p 150)*

Best **Kid-Friendly Hotel**
Hôtel Lion d'Or $$ *5 rue de la Sourdière, 1st (p 148)*

Best **Budget Sleep**
★ St Christopher's Inn $
159 rue de Crimée, 19th (p 152)

Best **Luxury Hotel**
★★★ Hôtel Shangri-Là $$$$$
10 av. d'léna, 16th (p 148)

Best **21st-Century Luxury**
★★★ Hyatt Regency Paris Madeleine $$$$$ *24 bd. Malesherbes, 8th (p 150)*

Best **Hip Hotel**
★★ Mama Shelter $$ *107 rue de Bagnolet, 20th (p 151)*

Best **Eco-Friendly Hotel**
Solar Hôtel $ *22 rue Boulard, 14th (p 152)*

Best **Family-Run Hôtel**
★★★ Hôtel Aviatic $$$
105 rue de Vaugirard, 6th (p 144)

Best **for Literary Types**
★ Hotel Lenox $$ *9 rue de l'Université, 7th (p 148)*

Best **"Only in Paris" Hideaway**
★★ Les Marroniers $$
78 rue d'Assas, 6th (p 151)

Best **Place to Detox**
★ Hotel Gabriel $$$ *25 rue du Grand Prieuré, 11th (p 147)*

Best **for Foodies**
Le Thoumieux $$$ *79 rue St-Dominique, 7th (p 150)*

Best **Beautiful B&B**
B&B Wonderful Paris $$ *52 rue de Clichy, 9th (p 149)*

Lodging Tip

The following prices don't cover Internet discounts. Always check the hotels' websites for special offers. Discount travel sites, such as www.booking.com, www.expedia.com, and www.venere.com, offer deals on select hotels. When choosing on these sites, avoid areas outside the city center by checking the arrondissement (district): Make sure the postcodes are from 75001 to 75020. Areas 1 (75001) to 8 (75008) are very central; 9 to 11 and 17 to 20 are the city's trendifying quarters; 12 to 16 are largely residential but have plenty of atmosphere. 13 contains the city's main Chinese quarter.

Previous page: The Hôtel Chopin in the Passage Jouffroy.

Right Bank (8th & 16th–18th)

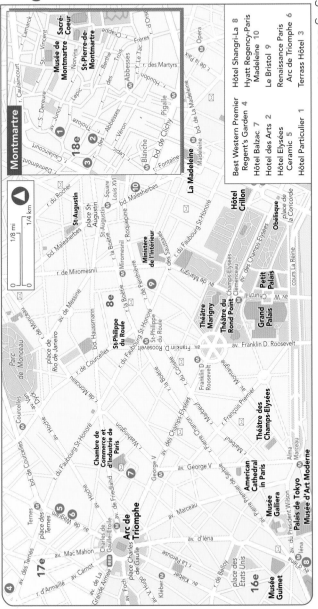

Best Western Premier
Regent's Garden 4
Hôtel Balzac 7
Hôtel des Arts 2
Hôtel Elysées
Ceramic 5
Hôtel Particulier 1

Hôtel Shangri-La 8
Hyatt Regency-Paris
Madeleine 10
Le Bristol 9
Renaissance Paris
Arc de Triomphe 6
Terrass Hôtel 3

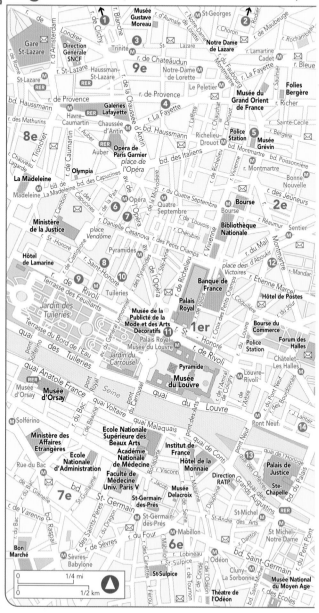

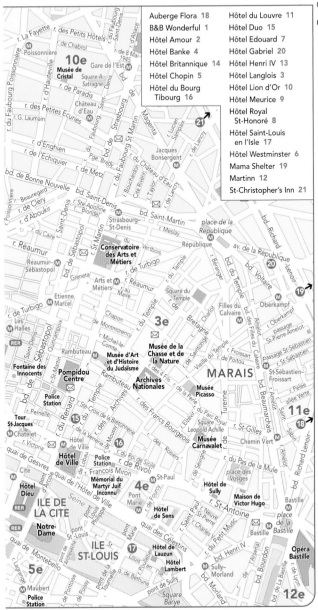

Auberge Flora 18
B&B Wonderful 1
Hôtel Amour 2
Hôtel Banke 4
Hôtel Britannique 14
Hôtel Chopin 5
Hôtel du Bourg Tibourg 16

Hôtel du Louvre 11
Hôtel Duo 15
Hôtel Edouard 7
Hôtel Gabriel 20
Hôtel Henri IV 13
Hôtel Langlois 3
Hôtel Lion d'Or 10
Hôtel Meurice 9
Hôtel Royal St-Honoré 8
Hôtel Saint-Louis en l'Isle 17
Hôtel Westminster 6
Mama Shelter 19
Martinn 12
St-Christopher's Inn 21

Left Bank (5th–6th)

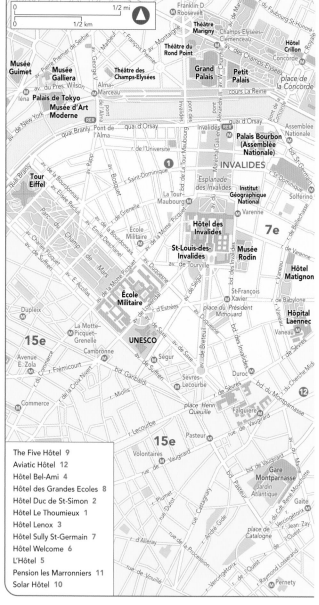

0 ____ 1/2 mi
0 ____ 1/2 km

Franklin D. Roosevelt Ⓜ

r. du Faubourg St-Honoré

Théâtre Marigny

Champs-Elysees-Clémenceau Ⓜ

av. de Marigny

Hôtel Crillon

r. Royale

Théâtre du Rond Point

av. des Champs-Elysées

Concorde Ⓜ

Musée Guimet

av. Pierre Premier de Serbie

r. Marbeuf

r. François Premier

av. George V

av. Montaigne

Théâtre des Champs-Elysées

Grand Palais

Petit Palais

place de la Concorde

Musée Galliera

av. du Prés. Wilson

Alma-Marceau Ⓜ

av. W. Churchill

cours La Reine

pont de la Concorde

Iéna Ⓜ

Palais de Tokyo

Musée d'Art Moderne

av. New York

pont de l'Alma

pont des Invalides

pont Alexandre III

quai d'Orsay

Assemblée Nationale

quai Branly

Pont de l'Alma

RER

quai d'Orsay

Invalides RER

Palais Bourbon (Assemblée Nationale)

bd. St-Germain

r. de l'Université

Maréchal Galliéni

INVALIDES

r. St-Dominique

Tour Eiffel

av. de la Bourdonnais

av. Elisée Réclus

r. Saint-Dominique

Esplanade des Invalides

Institut Géographique National

Solférino Ⓜ

La Tour-Maubourg Ⓜ

Varenne Ⓜ

7e

Parc du Champ de Mars

av. de la Bourdonnais

r. de Grenelle

Ecole Militaire

av. de la Motte Picquet

Hôtel des Invalides

Musée Rodin

r. de Bellechasse

r. de Varenne

av. Charles Floquet

av. de Suffren

r. Emile Deschanel

av. E. Acollas

av. de la Motte Picquet

St-Louis-des-Invalides

av. de Tourville

bd. des Invalides

Hôtel Matignon

r. Vaneau

École Militaire

av. de Lowendal

r. d'Estrées

place du Président Mithouard

St-François Xavier Ⓜ

r. de Babylone

Hôpital Laennec

Duplex Ⓜ

La Motte-Picquet-Grenelle Ⓜ

av. de Suffren

UNESCO

av. de Saxe

av. de Breteuil

bd. des Invalides

Vaneau Ⓜ

15e

Cambronne Ⓜ

av. de Ségur

Avenue E. Zola Ⓜ

r. du Commerce

r. Frémicourt

bd. Garibaldi

Ségur Ⓜ

Sèvres-Lecourbe Ⓜ

Duroc Ⓜ

r. de Sèvres

bd. du Montparnasse

r. du Cherche Midi

Commerce Ⓜ

r. de la Croix Nivert

r. Miollis

place Henri Queuille

Falguière Ⓜ

⑫

r. Lecourbe

Pasteur Ⓜ

rue de Vaugirard

av. du Maine

Volontaires Ⓜ

rue de Vaugirard

15e

bd. de Vaugirard

Gare Montparnasse

r. Plumet

r. Dutot

r. Castagnary

r. Pasteur

Jardin Atlantique

Gaîté Ⓜ

r. André Gide

place de Catalogne

av. du Cdt René Mouchotte

Jean Zay

r. d'Alleray

rue de la Procession

r. Vercingétorix

r. de l'Ouest

r. Raymond Losserand

Pernety Ⓜ

rue de Vouillé

Legend

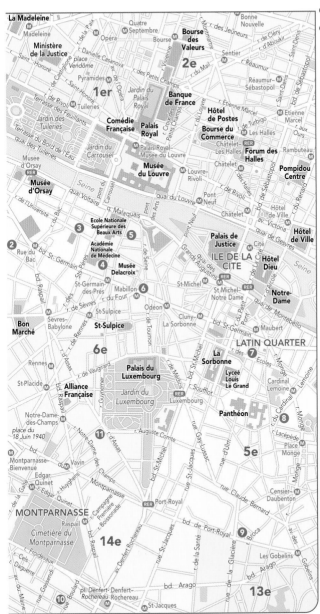

Hotels A to Z

★ **Auberge Flora** BASTILLE
This restaurant with rooms is a food lover's dream: Owner Flora Mikula was sous-chef to Alain Passard, and the quality and inventiveness of her dishes bear testiment to her training. Room-wise, expect bright colors, bold-patterned wallpaper, funky antiques, and textured fabrics. A great spot for exploring Bastille's market on Thursday and Sunday mornings (p 87). *44 bd. Richard Lenoir, 11th.* ☎ *01-47-00-52-77. www.aubergeflora.fr. 21 units. Double 200€–350€. MC, V. Métro: Richard Lenoir or Bréguet Sabin. Map p 140.*

★★★ **kids Aviatic Hotel** MONT-PARNASSE/SAINT-GERMAIN
Rooms in this family-run hotel are lushly decorated in thick, patterned fabrics and parquet floors. The hearty breakfasts are served in a bistro-style room that feels like a Left Bank institution. Families are welcome here, but the atmospheric is nonetheless romantic, too. *105 rue Vaugirard, 6th.* ☎ *01-53-63-25-50. www.aviatichotel.com. 42 units. Double 295€–360€ (up to 50% with online booking via hotel web-*site). *AE, MC, V. Métro: Montparnasse or St-Placide. Map p 142.*

★★★ **kids Best Western Premier Regent's Garden** CHAMPS-ELYSEES A good, guilt-free night's sleep is guaranteed in this environmentally friendly hotel, whose efforts to reduce carbon emissions have earned it the difficult-to-obtain European Ecolabel. Rooms are elegant, in bold stripes and patterns; there's a relaxing spa and a flower-filled courtyard—perfect for breakfast alfresco. *6 rue Pierre Demours, 8th.* ☎ *01-45-74-07-30. www.hotel-regents-paris.com. 40 units. Double 290€–440€. AE, MC, V. Métro: Ternes or Charles de Gaulle–Etoile. Map p 139.*

The Five Hôtel LATIN QUATER
The ultramodern rooms here are small but impressive, with Chinese lacquer, velvet fabrics, fiber-optic lighting that makes you feel as though you're sleeping under a starry sky, and your own room fragrance. In all, it's a fine design hotel and convenient base for exploring the Left Bank. *3 rue Flatters, 5th.* ☎ *01-43-31-74-21. www.*

The Aviatic Hotel in Saint-Germain is family-friendly yet romantic.

The Hôtel Banke is lodged in—you guessed it—a former bank building.

thefivehotel.com. 24 units. Double 101€–350€. MC, V. Métro: Les Gobelins. RER: Port Royal. Map p 140.

★ **Hôtel Amour** PIGALLE Rooms in this boutique hotel are individually decorated by progressive artists, such as Sophie Calle, M&M, and Pierre Le Tan. The result in some is risqué (photos of bare bottoms), but if you mind, what are you doing in Pigalle? The brasserie-bar with a hidden garden is a hit with Paris's trendy crowd. *8 rue Navarin, 9th.* 01-48-78-31-80. www.hotel amourparis.fr. 20 units. Double 165€–265€. AE, MC, V. Métro: Pigalle or St Georges. Map p 140.

★★ **Hôtel Balzac** CHAMPS-ELYSEES This Belle Epoque mansion with a pretty courtyard is luxuriously designed with ostentatious 19th-century touches and king-size beds. Its elegant restaurant is a hit with locals, who come for its comparably low prices (45€ a head) and intimate atmosphere. *6 rue Balzac, 8th.* 01-44-35-18-00. www.hotel balzac.com. 70 units. Double 400€–870€. AE, DC, MC, V. Métro: George-V. Map p 139.

★ **Hôtel Banke** OPERA This smart hotel has a breathtaking neo–Belle Epoque lobby, left over from a time when the building was a bank (hence the name). Rooms are stylish in browns and reds, and beds have ultracomfy mattresses. The restaurant offers a menu with a Spanish twist. *20 rue Lafayette, 9th.* 01-55-33-22-22. www.derby hotels.com. 94 units. Double 250€–500€. AE, MC, V. Métro: Le Peletier. Map p 140.

★ **Hôtel Bel-Ami** LATIN QUARTER Recently restored, this sleek, arts-conscious hotel has a minimalist look with a clean design aesthetic. Earth-tone guest rooms have a Zen-like air. Check the website for deals. *7–11 rue St-Benoit, 6th.* 01-49-27-09-33. www.hotel-bel-ami.com. 115 units. Double 270€–450€. AE, DC, MC, V. Métro: St-Germain-des-Prés. Map p 140.

★ **Hôtel Britannique** HOTEL DE VILLE Tastefully modern and plush, this place has cultivated a kind of English graciousness. Guest rooms are small but nicely appointed and soundproof. The location is so central, you can walk almost anywhere. *20 av. Victoria, 1st.* 01-42-33-74-59. www.hotel-britannique.com. 39 units. Double 218€–300€. AE, DC, MC, V. Métro: Châtelet. Map p 140.

★ **Hôtel Chopin** GRANDS BOULEVARDS This intimate, eccentric hotel is hidden inside a curious 19th-century covered passage. The Victorian lobby has elegant woodwork, rooms are comfortably furnished, and the staff is friendly. *10 bd. Montmartre, 9th.* 01-47-70-58-10. www.hotelchopin.fr. 36 units. Double 98€–118€. Métro: Grands Boulevards. Map p 142.

Hôtel des Arts MONTMARTRE Rooms in this old-fashioned but utterly charming hotel are simple,

Camille Pissaro once lived in the palatial building that houses the Hôtel du Louvre.

but some look out over Montmartre's rooftops. You couldn't ask for a better spot for exploring La Butte, its galleries, and its cobbled, hilly streets. *5 rue Tholozé, 18th.* ☎ *01-46-06-30-52. www.arts-hotel-paris.com. 50 units. Double 130€–195€. MC, V. Métro: Abbesses or Blanche. Map p 139.*

★★ Hôtel des Grandes Ecoles

LATIN QUARTER   This country house—with its old-fashioned floral wallpaper, chintz, and lace—looks amiss in Paris. The bucolic feel continues in the flower-filled garden, where noisy traffic dissolves into the twittering of birds—the perfect place for a lazy breakfast. Rooms are a good size and spotlessly clean. The welcome is friendly. *75 rue Cardinal Lemoine, 5th.* ☎ *01-43-26-79-23. www.hotel-grandes-ecoles.com. 51 units. Double 120€–150€. MC, V. Métro: Cardinal Lemoine. Map p 142.*

★ Hôtel du Bourg Tibourg

MARAIS   Hotels with far less style can cost twice as much as this well-located place. Rooms are small but comfortable, with romantic modern decor and lush fabrics in everything from leopard print to stripes. *19 rue du Bourg-Tibourg, 4th.* ☎ *01-42-78-47-39. www.hoteldubourgtibourg.com. 30 units. Double 270€–380€. AE, MC, V. Métro: Hôtel-de-Ville. Map p 140.*

★★ Hôtel du Louvre LOUVRE

This former home of painter Camille Pissarro is now a sort of Belle Epoque palace hotel, resplendent with marble, bronze, and gilt galore. Guest rooms are replete with antiques and heavy fabrics. *Place André Malraux, 1st.* ☎ *01-44-58-38-38. www.hoteldulouvre.com. 177 units. Double 455€–650€. AE, DC, MC, V. Métro: Palais Royal or Louvre Rivoli. Map p 139.*

★ Hôtel Duc de St-Simon

INVALIDES   A sweet courtyard offers your first glimpse of this hopelessly romantic hotel that has seduced the likes of Lauren Bacall. Rooms are filled with antiques, objets d'art, and lush fabrics. Some have terraces overlooking a garden. *14 rue de St-Simon, 7th.* ☎ *01-44-39-20-20. www.hotelducdesaintsimon.com. 34 units. Double 275€–315€. AE, MC, V. Métro: Rue du Bac. Map p 140.*

★★ Hôtel-Duo MARAIS   One of

the city's trendiest cutting-edge hotels, with a location right in the heart of the Marais. Decor has an old-world charm with a distinctly modern feel thanks to rooms all dressed up in cool browns, creams, and bold-print wallpaper. *11 rue du Temple, 4th.* ☎ *01-42-72-72-22. www.duo-paris.com. 45 units. Double 250€–380€. AE, DC, MC, V. Métro: Hôtel-de-Ville. Map p 140.*

★★ Hôtel Edouard 7 OPERA

The Edouard 7's balcony views over the Opéra Garnier are breathtaking. The hotel is also in a plum location for shopping at the Galeries Lafayette department store and visiting the Louvre. The large and airy rooms come in two designs: "Classical," with antique furniture; and "Couture," in warm-tone velvets, rather like a boudoir. *39 av. de l'Opéra, 2nd.* ☎ *01- 42-61-56-90. www.edouard7hotel.com. 69 units. Double 350€–450€. AE, DC, MC, V. Métro: Opéra. RER Auber. Map p 139.*

★ Hôtel Elysées Ceramic

ETOILE An ornate ceramic facade helps make this celebrated Art Nouveau building easy to find. The clean, modern, attractive rooms are less over the top; the shaded patio is a godsend in summer. *34 av. de Wagram, 8th.* ☎ *01-42-27-20-30. www.elysees-ceramic.com. 57 units. Double 237€. AE, DC, MC, V. Métro: Charles-de-Gaulle-Etoile. Map p 139.*

★ Hôtel Gabriel REPUBLIQUE

Relaxing massages, healthy food, and Zen decor are what you get at Paris's first-ever detox hotel. Come here to wind down and escape the city life outside. *25 rue du Grand Prieuré, 11th.* ☎ *01-47-00-13-38. www.gabrielparismarais.com. 40 units.*

Hôtel Langlois features Belle Epoque architectural details and moderate rates.

Double 120€–280€. Métro: République. Map p 140.

★★★ Hôtel Henri IV THE

ISLANDS This is possibly Paris's best budget hotel, at the heart of the Île de la Cité, near Notre-Dame and pont Neuf. Rooms are very basic but clean, and the top-floor rooms have balconies. Book way in advance. Only 11 rooms have en suite bathrooms with toilets. The sandy square just in front is a perfect spot for a game of *boules. 25 place Dauphine, 1st.* ☎ *01-43-54-44-53. www.henri4hotel.fr. 15 units. Double 77€–87€. MC, V. Métro: Pont Neuf. Map p 140.*

★ Hôtel Langlois GRANDS

BOULEVARDS This charming hotel in a restored town house has

Guests' health and well-being come first at the Hôtel Gabriel.

such charming touches as a curving Parisian stairwell and an antique wrought-iron elevator. Rooms are smallish but tasteful, some with fireplaces. *63 rue St-Lazare, 9th.* ☎ *01-48-74-78-24. www.hotel-langlois.com. 27 units. Double 180€–190€. AE, DC, MC, V. Métro: Trinité. Map p 139.*

★ **Hotel Lenox** SAINT-GERMAIN-DES-PRES   The staff will happily fill you in on the literary history of the hotel. (T.S. Eliot convinced James Joyce to stay here after Ezra Pound fell in love with the place.) The bar alone is worth a visit. The modern guest rooms, reached via a glass elevator, are decorated in creamy tones with rich blue accents and some antique reproductions. Some rooms have wondrous views. *9 rue de l'Université, 7th.* ☎ *01-42-96-10-95. www.lenoxsaintgermain.com. 40 units. Double 138€–270€. AE, DC, MC, V. Métro: St-Germain-des-Prés. Map p 140.*

★★ **kids** **Hôtel Lion d'Or** TUILERIES   The "Golden Lion" has bright, simple rooms plus fully furnished apartments that sleep up to five people. It's well located, too, right near the Louvre. *5 rue de la Sourdière, 1st.* ☎ *01-42-60-79-04. www.hotel-louvre-paris.com. 27 units. Double 136€–200€, apt 280€–490€. MC, V. Métro: Tuileries. Map p 139.*

★★ **Hôtel Meurice** CONCORDE   Salvador Dalí once made this hotel his headquarters. It's gorgeous, with perfectly preserved mosaic floors, hand-carved moldings, and an Art Nouveau glass roof. Rooms are sumptuous and individually decorated, some with fluffy clouds and blue skies painted on the ceilings. *228 rue de Rivoli, 1st.* ☎ *01-44-58-10-10. www.meuricehotel.com. 160 units. Double 640€–830€. AE, DC, MC, V. Métro: Tuileries or Concorde. Map p 139.*

★★★ **Hôtel Particulier** MONT-MARTRE   You'll be hard-pressed to find somewhere more romantic or stylish than this hidden gem, nestled down a leafy passage by a rock called Rocher de la Sorcière (Witch's Rock). Avant-garde artists have given each room a special touch. *23 av. Junot, 18th.* ☎ *01-53-41-81-40. www.hotel-particulier-montmartre.com. 5 units. Double 312€–590€. MC, V. Métro: Lamarck-Caulincourt. Map p 139.*

★★ **Hôtel Royal St-Honoré** CONCORDE   This oasis of charm attracts guests drawn by nearby shops, such as Chanel and Hermès. Contemporary styling contrasts nicely with antique furnishings. The bar is *très* chic. *221 rue St-Honoré, 1st.* ☎ *01-42-60-32-79. www.hotel-royal-st-honore.com. 72 units. Double 170€–350€ w/ breakfast. AE, DC, MC, V. Métro: Tuileries. Map p 139.*

★★★ **Hôtel Shangri-La** CHAILLOT   Set inside the 19th-century palace Napoleon built for his great-nephew Prince Roland Bonaparte, this hotel drips with fine furniture, chandeliers, and antiques. But there's a modern edge, too, in the classy rooms, lounge, and two superlative eateries: **L'Abeille** for

Contemporary artwork, sumptuous decor, and a secluded garden are the draws at the Hôtel Particulier.

Bed & Breakfasts in Paris

For a special, intimate Parisian experience, consider booking a B&B. Here are some reliable places to try: **Alcôve & Agapes** (☎ 01-44-85-06-05; www.bed-and-breakfast-in-paris.com), with more than 100 regularly inspected addresses throughout central Paris; **Hôtes Qualité Paris** (www.hotesqualiteparis.fr), which has an excellent, trustworthy selection verified by City Hall; and **Alastair Sawday's** (www.sawdays.co.uk), which lists many special B&Bs and apartments to rent. To live like a local in trendy SoPi (south Pigalle, below Montmartre), try **B&B Wonderful,** 52 rue de Clichy, 9th (☎ 06-66-01-75-44; www.facebook.com/BnBWonderfulParis; from 115€), a fabulous B&B for two, with a separate flat that sleeps up to four people. Breakfast is copious; the balcony views over Paris's steely rooftops picturesque; and the welcome, by expat owner Rosemary, perfect. She can even give you a makeover (prices on request), as she's an image consultant by trade.

---

haute French cuisine (p 112) and **La Bauhinia** brasserie, which mixes Asian and French flavors. *10 av. d'Iéna, 16th.* ☎ *01-53-67-19-98. www.shangri-la.com. 81 units. Double 870€–950€. AE, DC, MC, V. Métro: Iéna. Map p 139.*

★ Hôtel St-Louis en l'Isle

ÎLE ST-LOUIS   A charming family atmosphere reigns at this antiques-filled hotel in a 17th-century town house. Rooms are small but well decorated, there are lots of lovely touches, and the location is excellent. Great value for the price. *75 rue St-Louis-en-l'Île, 4th.* ☎ *01-46-34-04-80. www.hotelsaintlouis.com. 19 units. Double 175€–245€. MC, V. Métro: Pont Marie or St-Michel-Notre-Dame. Map p 140.*

★ Hôtel Sully St-Germain

LATIN QUARTER   With its neo-medieval decor and exquisite antiques, this is a good option for the money. Stylish guest rooms have brass beds and stone walls. *31 rue des Ecoles, 5th.* ☎ *01-43-26-56-02. www.hotel-paris-sully.com. 61 units. Double 157€–265€. AE, DC,* MC, V. Métro: Maubert Mutualité. Map p 140.

★★ Hôtel Welcome

SAINT-GERMAIN-DES-PRES   Nestled among the art galleries and cafes of Saint-Germain, this quaint hotel oozes atmosphere, with wooden beams, old furniture, classic red and cream drapes, and street views from most bedrooms. A real steal for such a good Left Bank location. *66 rue de Seine, 6th.* ☎ *01-46-34-24-80. www.hotelwelcomeparis.com. 29 units. Double 107€–240€. MC, V. Métro: St-Germain-des-Prés or Odéon. Map p 140.*

★★★ Hôtel Westminster

OPERA   This gorgeous hotel is favored by shoppers who prowl Place Vendôme, Rue du Faubourg Saint-Honoré, and the department stores around Opéra Garnier for chic attire. Decor is resolutely stylish: classic marbles, deep woods, and plush fabrics. The Michelin-starred restaurant is known for its fine contemporary French cuisine. *13 rue de la Paix, 2nd.* ☎ *01-42-61-57-46. www.*

warwickwestminsteropera.com. 102 units. Double 230€–650€. AE, MC, V. Métro: Opéra. RER: Auber. Map p 139.

Hyatt Regency Paris-Madeleine

MADELEINE   This palace hotel is a citadel of luxurious 21st-century living. High ceilings and neo–Art Deco touches make the hotel airy and dramatic. The sleek fittings add to the luxury, as do the rich fabrics and precious wooden furniture. *24 bd. Malesherbes, 8th.* ☎ *01-55-27-15-34. www.paris.madeleine.hyatt. com/hyatt/hotels. 86 units. Double 300€–700€. AE, DC, MC, V. Métro: St-Augustin. Map p 139.*

★★★ kids Le Bristol

CHAMPS-ELYSEES   Paris's most discreet palace hotel is a favorite with celebrities, politicians, and royalty. Guest rooms are lavish, large, and luxurious. The swimming pool has views over the whole city. The 3-Michelin-starred restaurant, Epicure, opens onto Paris's biggest palace garden (1,500 sq. m/16,000 sq. ft.) in the summer; and its 1-starred 114 Faubourg brasserie is well worth crossing Paris for. If you can't afford a room, observe the glitterati over a cocktail in the bar. You might even meet Fa-raon, the resident cat—he's a hit with kids. *112 rue du Faubourg St-Honoré, 8th.* ☎ *01-53-43-43-00. www.hotel-bristol.com. 170 units. Double*

The palatial yet discreet hotel Le Bristol.

800€–2,200€. AE, DC, MC, V. Métro: Franklin-D.-Roosevelt. Map p 139.

★ L'Hôtel

SAINT-GERMAIN-DES-PRES   The hotel where Oscar Wilde died is now one of the Left Bank's most distinctive boutique hotels. Each guest room is different, some with fireplaces, some with fabric-covered walls. There's a swimming pool in the cellar, and the restaurant (p 109) is one of the best in town. *13 rue des Beaux-Arts, 6th.* ☎ *01-44-41-99-00. www.l-hotel. com. 20 units. Double 255€–660€. AE, DC, MC, V. Métro: St-Germain-des-Prés. Map p 140.*

★★★ Il Hôtel Thoumieux

INVALIDES   Jean-François Piège is a celebrity chef in France, and this chic neo-'70s-style hotel is his most recent lair. The rooms (all in turquoises, animal print) sit discreetly above his restaurants—the gastronomic **Restaurant Jean-François Piège** (p 111), and the **Thoumieux Brasserie** (p 107)—which means you only have to stumble upstairs after dinner. The problem is that both are so good, and the rooms so cozy, you might never go anywhere else in Paris! *79 rue St-Dominique, 7th.* ☎ *01-47-05-79-00. www. thoumieux.fr. 15 units. Double 225€–450€. AE, MC, V. Métro: La Tour Maubourg. Map p 142.*

The young and stylish flock to Mama Shelter, in the 20th arrondissement.

★★ **Mama Shelter** PERE-LACHAISE   Rooms in this starkly modern design hotel, set in a converted car park, are full of fun touches, such as lights made of superhero Halloween masks and 24" wall-mounted iMacs with TV, radio, and web access. Downstairs, a bar, pizza parlor, and restaurant draw a crowd of international trendies. It's the place to see and be seen. *107 rue de Bagnolet, 20th.* ☎ *01-43-48-48-48. www.mamashelter.com. 170 units. Double 79€–409€. MC, V. Métro: Alexandre Dumas or Porte de Bagnolet. Map p 139.*

★★ **Martinn** SENTIER   This self-catering one-bedroom apartment is the sort of place you wished you owned: Heavy doors open onto a lovely taffeta-clad bedroom, an airy living area, and a kitchen that cries out to be cooked in. Cooking classes and wine tastings are available on request. *62 rue d'Argout, 2nd.* ☎ *06-23-55-34-82. www.key2paris.com. 1 unit. From 770€ per week. MC, V. Métro: Sentier. Map p 140.*

★★★ **Pension les Marronniers** LUXEMBOURG   This is one of the city's very last *pensions de famille* (boarding houses)—perfect for nostalgic travelers looking for a slice of bygone Paris. It has been in the owner's family since the 1930s and offers great views over the Luxembourg Gardens. Rooms are cluttered—just as they should be. Half-board is available. *78 rue d'Assas, 6th.* ☎ *01-43-26-37-71. www.pension-marronniers.com. 7 units. Double 94€–140€. No credit cards. Weekly and monthly rentals. Métro: Notre-Dame des Champs or Vavin Map p 142.*

★★ **Renaissance Paris Arc de Triomphe** CHAMPS-ELYSEES   Order a Paris Sky View Room and watch the Eiffel Tower twinkle from your balcony in this trendy 5-star hotel. It has elegantly modern architecture, and if you fancy non-French cuisine, the Macassar restaurant serves scrumptious Indonesian-inspired dishes like *ikan dabu dabu* (roasted marinated swordfish with basmati rice and sauce vierge). *39 av. de Wagram, 17th. 01-55-37-55-37. www.marriott.com. 118 units. Double from 469€–700€. MC, V. Métro: Ternes. Map p 139.*

The St-Christopher's Inn youth hostel chain recently opened a second Paris location, at 5 rue de Dunkerque.

The charming dining room at the Pension les Marronniers boarding house.

★★★ **Solar Hôtel** DENFERT-ROCHEREAU   Paris's first low-budget environmentally friendly hotel has a fabulous concept: Modern rooms without frills but with A/C, TV, and phones; a pretty garden where you can picnic and hire bikes; static prices year-round; and a genuine low-carbon charter. *22 rue Boulard, 14th.* ☎ *01-43-21-08-20. www.solarhotel.fr. 34 units. Double 69€. MC, V. Métro/RER: Denfert-Rochereau. Map p 142.*

St-Christopher's Inn STALINGRAD   This English youth hostel chain, set inside an old boat hangar, has funky decor and unbeatable prices. Private rooms and dormers are marine-themed. Dorms are single-sex and mixed, so check when you book. *159 rue de Crimée, 19th.* ☎ *01-40-34-34-40. www.st-christophers.co.uk. 350 beds. Dorm 33€ (occasional special offers), double 48€–60€. Métro: Crimée. Map p 139.*

★ **Terrass Hôtel** MONTMARTRE This hotel is a find, with a marble-floored lobby, blond-oak paneling, antiques, and paintings. Guest rooms have high ceilings and sophisticated decor. The rooftop bar is coveted by Parisians for its uninterrupted views, which include the Eiffel Tower. *12 rue Joseph de Maistre, 18th.* ☎ *01-46-06-72-85. www.terrass-hotel.com. 100 units. Double 345€–450€. Métro: Place de Clichy or Blanche. Map p 139.* ●

Decadent Versailles

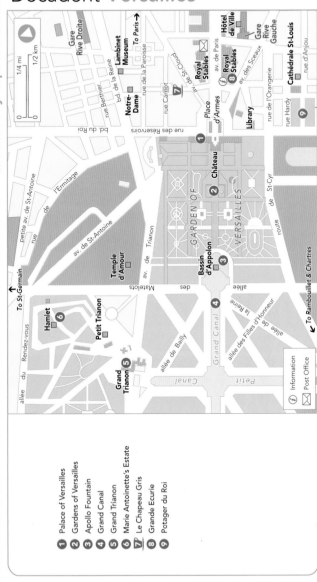

1 Palace of Versailles
2 Gardens of Versailles
3 Apollo Fountain
4 Grand Canal
5 Grand Trianon
6 Marie Antoinette's Estate
7 Le Chapeau Gris
8 Grande Ecurie
9 Potager du Roi

Previous page: The Sun King's Hall of Mirrors reflects natural light back into the garden at Versailles.

Yes, it's touristy, and yes, it will be crowded in the summer, but come anyway. Versailles must be seen to be believed, and it is well worth the 35-minute journey. It took 40,000 workers 50 years to convert Louis XIII's hunting lodge into this extravagant palace. The major work was started in 1678 by Jules Hardouin Mansart under Louis XIV, and before it was finished, entire forests had been moved to make way for its extensive gardens. It was here in the 18th century that French royalty lived a life of such excess in a time of widespread poverty that it spurred a revolution.

❶ ★★★ Palace of Versailles.
One of the first things you'll notice when you arrive is that this vast palace of 2,300 rooms is dwarfed by the grounds, which stretch for miles. Inside the palace, it's all over-the-top, all the time. The king and his family lived in the Petits Appartements much of the time, where the king's apartment and the queen's bedchamber are exquisitely overdone. One room, the Cabinet of the Meridian, was where Marie Antoinette finally gave birth to an heir in 1781, after 11 years of marriage. The King's Grand Appartement is actually an enfilade of seven terrifically decked-out rooms—showpieces for visitors to the court. The largest is the Hercules Salon, where the ceiling is painted with the *Apotheosis of Hercules*. The elaborate Mercury Salon is where the body of Louis XIV lay in state after his death. But the apartments pale in comparison to the 71m-long (233-ft.) Hall of Mirrors designed by Mansart. The Hall of Mirrors was designed to reflect sunlight back into the garden and remind people that the "Sun King" lived here. On June 28, 1919, the treaty ending World War I was signed in this hall. Elsewhere in the palace there's an impressive Clock Room, designed in 1753 by architect Jacques-Ange Gabriel, with a gilded-bronze astronomical clock that is supposed to keep perfect time until 9999. 🕐 *2 hr.*

❷ ★★★ Gardens of Versailles.
These vast, varied, vainglorious gardens were created by the landscape architect André Le Nôtre, who used lakes, canals, geometric flower beds, long avenues, fountains, and statuary to devise a French Eden. Thousands of men moved tons of soil, trees, and rock for the plan. The result—beautifully maintained for hundreds of years—is simply breathtaking. 🕐 *2 hr.*

❸ Apollo Fountain. At one time, hundreds of fountains burbled around the grounds. The most famous surviving example is the

The courtyard of Versailles.

The gardens of Versailles nearly outdo the palace itself.

Apollo fountain (created in 1670 by Jean-Baptiste Tuby after a drawing by Charles Le Brun), which depicts Apollo's chariot.

④ **Grand Canal.** The 1.6km (1-mile) canal is surrounded by lush planted forests crossed by straight paths. So precise was Le Nôtre's design that on St. Louis Day (Aug 25), the sun sets in perfect alignment with the Grand Canal.

⑤ ★★ **Grand Trianon.** The elegant Grand Trianon was designed in 1687 by Jules Hardouin Mansart. It was later the home of Napoleon and his family. Then, in 1963, President Charles de Gaulle had it turned into a guesthouse for French presidents. The northern wing, the Trianon-sous-Bois, is still used today for presidential functions. ⏱ *30 min.*

⑥ **Marie Antoinette's Estate.** Louis XVI's young wife is famed for her desire to flee the pomp of the Versailles court. Her retreat was this estate—made up of the Queen's Gardens, the **Hameau de la Reine** (a lovely thatch-roofed hamlet of fanciful faux farmhouses), and the **Petit Trianon** (a perfectly scaled gem of a building that architecture buffs flip for, it was also a meeting place for Louis XV and Madame de Pompadour). ⏱ *30 min.*

Travel Tip

Both the Grand Trianon and Marie Antoinette's estate can be reached by the "Petit Train" from the Parterre Nord (☎ 01-39-54-22-00; www.train-versailles.com; 6.90€). The round trip is narrated by a guide and takes 50 minutes, but you can hop on and hop off at each site.

⑦ **Le Chapeau Gris.** Stop for a bite of French country cuisine in Versailles's oldest restaurant, whose building (with paneled walls and beamed ceilings) dates back to the construction of the château. The prix-fixe menus, at 23€ and 30€, are excellent values. *7 rue Hoche.* ☎ *01-39-50-10-81. www.auchapeaugris.com. $$.*

The Pomp of Versailles Gardens

Each weekend between April and November, the palace's fountains spurt to the rhythms of Baroque music during the 60- to 90-minute **Grandes Eaux Musicales,** a wonderful exhibition that takes you back to the time of the Sun King. Every Tuesday between April and October (except June) sees classical music fill Le Nôtre's landscaped patchworks (from 10:30am–6pm) during **Les Jardins Musicaux.**

Versailles: Practical Matters

Versailles (☎ 01-30-83-78-00; www.châteauversailles.fr) is open Tuesday through Sunday from 9am to 5:30pm (Apr–Oct until 6:30pm). The gardens are open daily year-round from 8am to 6pm (Apr–Oct until 8:30pm). Admission to the château is 13€ to 15€. Admission to the Grand Trianon and Marie Antoinette's estate is 6€ to 10€. Admission to the gardens is free (except during the Grandes Eaux, when it's 8€). However, the best and easiest way to visit Versailles is to buy a *Passeport Versailles* (18€–25€; free for children 17 and under and visitors 25 and under from the E.U., except during the Grandes Eaux and Jardins Musicaux events—see box p 156), which allows quick access to the main Château, the Grand Trianon, and Marie Antoinette's estate. Buy tickets online or at an FNAC (p 88). If you already have your ticket when you arrive, head straight to door A. To buy your ticket, head to the information/ticket point in the south wing. For tickets to the Grand Trianon and Marie Antoinette's estate, head straight to that entrance in the gardens.

There are two stations in Versailles—Rive Gauche (the nearest one to the château) and Rive Droite. To get to the former, take RER C from central Paris to Versailles–Rive Gauche; or take a normal train from Gare St-Lazare to Versailles–Rive Droite and then walk 10 minutes. By car, take the A-13 from Paris to the Versailles-Château exit. Pay parking is available on the Place d'Armes. The trip to Versailles takes about 30 to 40 minutes by car or train.

⑧ Grande Ecurie. The famous Versailles horses are kept in high style here and trained in a variety of equine performance arts (at the Académie du Spectacle Equestre). You can watch the horse trainers at work on Saturday, Sunday, and some Thursday mornings, or take in a performance or evenings (and some Thursdays). For times, check the website or call in advance. ⏱ *1 hr. 15 min. Near the palace entrance on av. Rockefeller.* ☎ *01-48-39-18-03. www.bartabas.fr. Admission 12€, performances 25€.*

⑨ Potager du Roi. This enclosure, made up of 5,000 fruit trees tapered into extravagant shapes, is where the Sun King's fruit and vegetable plot stood. The garden is now separate from the château and well worth visiting whether your thumbs are green or not. ⏱ *30 min. Access via Rue du Maréchal Joffr (left main entrance).* ☎ *01-39-24-62-62. www.potager-du-roi.fr. Admission 4.50€, free for children 12 & under. Apr–Oct Tues–Sun 10am–6pm; Jan–Mar Tues & Thurs 10am–1pm; Nov–Dec Tues & Thurs 10am–6pm, Sat 10am–1pm. Closed May 1 & during Christmas school holidays.*

Disneyland Paris

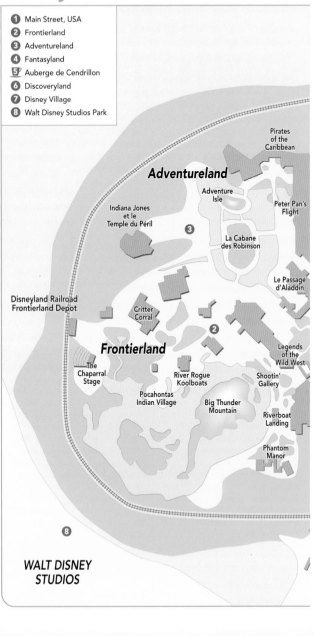

1. Main Street, USA
2. Frontierland
3. Adventureland
4. Fantasyland
5. Auberge de Cendrillon
6. Discoveryland
7. Disney Village
8. Walt Disney Studios Park

Pirates of the Caribbean

Adventureland

Adventure Isle

Peter Pan's Flight

Indiana Jones et le Temple du Péril

La Cabane des Robinson

Le Passage d'Aladdin

Disneyland Railroad Frontierland Depot

Critter Corral

Frontierland

Legends of the Wild West

The Chaparral Stage

River Rogue Koolboats

Shootin' Gallery

Pocahontas Indian Village

Big Thunder Mountain

Riverboat Landing

Phantom Manor

WALT DISNEY STUDIOS

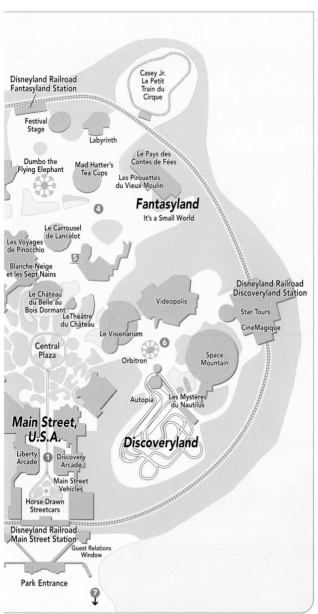

Disneyland Railroad
Fantasyland Station

Casey Jr.
Le Petit
Train du
Cirque

Festival
Stage

Labyrinth

Le Pays des
Contes de Fées

Dumbo the
Flying Elephant

Mad Hatter's
Tea Cups

Les Pirouettes
du Vieux Moulin

4

Fantasyland

It's a Small World

Le Carrousel
de Lancelot

Les Voyages
de Pinocchio

5

Blanche-Neige
et les Sept Nains

Le Château
du Belle au
Bois Dormant

Vidéopolis

Disneyland Railroad
Discoveryland Station

Star Tours

Le Théâtre
du Château

CinéMagique

Le Visionarium

Central
Plaza

6

Orbitron

Space
Mountain

Autopia

Les Mystères
du Nautilus

*Main Street,
U.S.A.*

Discoveryland

Liberty
Arcade

1

Discovery
Arcade

Main Street
Vehicles

Horse-Drawn
Streetcars

Disneyland Railroad
Main Street Station

Guest Relations
Window

Park Entrance

7
↓

Disneyland Paris is a blessing for travelers with kids who have wearied of the museums and churches and just want to go on the rides for 1 day, pleasepleaseplease! Overall, there's little difference between this amusement park and those in Florida and California, except here the cheeseburgers comes with *pommes frîtes* instead of fries. There are two main parks: Disneyland Park, with its five lands, and Walt Disney Studios Park, split into lots.

1 Main Street, USA. Immediately after entering the park, you'll find yourself in an idealized American town, complete with horse-drawn carriages and street-corner barbershop quartets. If you're here after dark, you can take in the surprisingly lovely Electric Parade (nightly July–Aug), when all the Disney characters pass by along with brightly illuminated floats.

2 Frontierland. In this "pretend America," it's a conveniently short hop to the West, particularly if you board one of the steam-powered trains that takes you through a Grand Canyon diorama to Frontierland. Pocahontas's Indian village is a fine spot to get young kids away from the crowds. If it gets too hot, you and the kids can ride the nearby paddle-wheel steamship.

3 Adventureland. The trains will take you on to Adventureland, where swashbuckling pirates battle near the Swiss Family Robinson's treehouse. If that's too tame, head for the Indiana Jones and the Temple of Peril ride. It travels backward at breakneck speed, the only Disneyland roller coaster in the world to do so.

4 Fantasyland. Young children will be charmed by Sleeping Beauty's Castle (*Le Château de la Belle au Bois Dormant*) and its idealized interpretation of a French château, complete with the obligatory fire-breathing dragon in its dungeon. From here, a visit with Dumbo the Flying Elephant may be necessary, and perhaps a whirl on the giant teacup ride.

Take in a fake lake at Disneyland Paris.

Disney Village is a haven for adults.

5 Auberge de Cendrillon. If you're looking for a nice sit-down lunch, try this restaurant for traditional French dining in Cinderella's country inn. (Reservations are recommended.) Otherwise, take your pick from any of the dozens of dining options scattered throughout the park—although don't expect high standards or healthy options. *Fantasyland.* ☎ 01-64-74-24-02. $$$.

6 Discoveryland. Explore the visions of the future displayed here, with designs drawn from the works of Leonardo da Vinci, Jules Verne, and H. G. Wells, as well as from more modern fictional creations, like the *Star Wars* universe. This is the park's most popular area, with its own version of Space Mountain, which emulates Jules Verne's version of what a trip from Earth to the moon would be like.

7 Disney Village. This haven for adults features endless entertainment options—dance clubs, snack bars, restaurants, shops, and bars. There's also a massive 3-D IMAX cinema, where you can see all the latest blockbusters.

8 Walt Disney Studios Park. Split into four lots (Toon Studio, Backlot, Front Lot, and Production Courtyard), the second park emphasizes film production and special effects. Feel the flames as you play an extra in the *Armageddon* disaster movie, plunge 13 floors down an elevator shaft in the Twilight Tower of Terror, or get your kids to talk live with the mischievous alien Stitch in his interactive stage show.

Disneyland Paris: Practical Matters

Drive 32km (20 miles) along the A4 east from Paris to exit 14. Or take the RER A to the Marne-la-Vallée–Chessy stop (about 40 min.) The park is at Marne-la-Vallée, Paris (☎ 08-25-30-02-22; www.disneylandparis.com). Parking is 15€ per day. Admission for 1-day (one park) is 62€ adults, 56€ ages 3–11, and free for children 2 and under; a 1-day hopper (both parks) is 74€ adults and 66€ ages 3–11. Disneyland Park is open September to mid-June Monday through Friday 10am to 8pm and Saturday through Sunday 10am to 9pm, and mid-June to August daily 10am to 11pm. Walt Disney Studios Park is open winter daily 10am to 6pm, and summer daily 10am to 7pm. (These are guidelines, and opening hours may change.) The resort was designed as a total vacation destination, so within the enormous compound there are not only the two parks but also six hotels, campgrounds, the Village Disney entertainment center, a 27-hole golf course, and dozens of restaurants and shops.

The Cathedral at Chartres

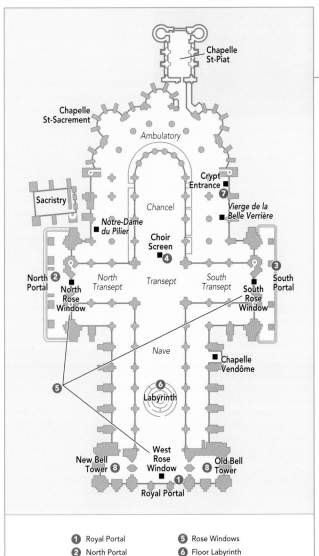

Chapelle
St-Piat

Chapelle
St-Sacrement

Ambulatory

Crypt
Entrance ■ ⑦

Chancel

*Vierge de la
Belle Verrière* ■

Sacristy

*Notre-Dame
du Pilier* ■

Choir
Screen
④

North ②
Portal

*North
Transept*

Transept

*South
Transept*

South
Rose
Window

③
South
Portal

North
Rose
Window

Nave

■ Chapelle
Vendôme

⑤

⑥
Labyrinth

New Bell
Tower ⑧

West
Rose
Window ■

⑧ Old Bell
Tower

① Royal Portal

①	Royal Portal	⑤	Rose Windows
②	North Portal	⑥	Floor Labyrinth
③	South Portal	⑦	Crypts
④	Choir Screen	⑧	Towers

An hour from Paris, standing at the gateway to the Loire Valley, Chartres represents the highest architectural and theological aspirations of the Middle Ages in France. The cathedral was much the same in medieval times as it is now, which should give you a sense of how impressive it must have been in 1260, when it was completed. Rodin described it as the French Acropolis, and once you've seen it, you'll be hard pressed to disagree with him.

1 Royal Portal. The sculpted bodies around it are elongated and garbed in long, flowing robes, but their faces are almost disturbingly lifelike—frowning, winking, and smiling. Christ is shown at the Second Coming—his descent to Earth on the right, his ascent back to Heaven on the left.

2 & 3 North and South Portals. Both the North Portal and the South Portals are carved with Biblical images, including the expulsion of Adam and Eve from the Garden of Eden.

4 Choir Screen. This celebrated screen dates to the 16th century. It has 40 niches holding statues of Biblical figures. Don't be so dazzled by all the stained glass (see next stop) that you overlook its intricate carvings.

5 ★★★ Rose Windows. No cathedral in the world can match Chartres for its 12th-century glass (saved from damage during World

One of the cathedral's magnificent rose windows.

War I and World War II by parishioners who removed it piece by piece and stored it safely). It gave the world a new color—Chartres blue—and it is absolutely exceptional. All the windows are glorious, but the three rose windows may be the best.

6 Floor Labyrinth. Many Gothic cathedrals once had labyrinths like the one on the floor of the nave,

A Special Place to Stay near Chartres

With its moat, forest walks, and 60 hectares (148 acres) of gardens, the Renaissance ★★ **Château d'Esclimont** is a fairy-tale place to stay and dine, between Chârtres and Paris, at St Symphorien Le Château (☎ 02-37-31-15-15; www.grandesetapes.fr; double rooms from 150€; 3-course meal 90€, lunch menu from 39€). The gourmet restaurant (think French classics like beef tournedos and lobster) overlooks the gardens. In good weather, you can even eat in a hot-air balloon while sailing over the forested countryside (from 1,340€ for in-flight dinner for two). Rooms are stately, with marble bathrooms and thick drapes.

Chartres: Practical Matters

From Paris's Gare Montparnasse, trains run directly to Chartres (1 hr.). By car, take A-10/A-11 southwest from the Périphérique and follow signs to Le Mans and Chartres (about 1½ hr.). The cathedral is open May through October daily from 8am to 8pm and November through April daily from 8am to 7:15pm. Admission is free. Audio guides are available for 6.20€. Guided tours of the cathedral are available in English twice a day (Easter–Oct) by lecturer Malcolm Miller at noon and 2:45pm Monday through Saturday (at noon only Nov–Easter if more than eight participants). Admission 10€. For tour information, inquire in the gift shop or contact Miller at ☎ 02-37-28-15-58 and millerchartres@aol.com. Cloître Notre-Dame, 28000, Chartres. ☎ 02-37-21-59-08. www.cathedrale-chartres.org.

Any trip to the cathedral should include a visit to the medieval cobbled streets of **Chartres's Vieux Quartier (Old Quarter),** which stretches from the cathedral down to the Eure River. **Rue Chantault,** where the 800-year-old houses have wonderfully colorful facades, is particularly lovely. Also, stop in at the **Musée des Beaux Arts de Chartres,** right next to the cathedral, at 29 Cloître Notre-Dame (☎ 02-37-90-45-80; admission 3.50€). It has an excellent collection covering the 16th through the 20th centuries. You'll find a vibrant food market Saturdays and Wednesday mornings in the market hall at Place Billard, near the cathedral. There's also a flower market Tuesdays, Thursdays, and Saturdays at Place du Cygne. For lunch, try **Le Saint-Hilaire,** 11 rue Pont St-Hilaire (☎ 02-37-30-97-57. www.restaurant-saint-hilaire.fr), a traditional French restaurant.

but virtually all were destroyed over time, but this one, which dates from around 1200, is very rare. It is thought that such labyrinths represented the passage of the soul to heaven. Its 261.5m (858-ft.) path was either walked in prayer as a symbolic pilgrimage to Jerusalem or as a path of repentance, in which case the sinner would cover the distance on his or her knees.

⑦ Crypts. Those who would like to visit the cathedral's underbelly can usually only do so as part of a guided tour in French (2.70€). Tag along even if your French is nonexistent to see the wondrous crypt, medieval frescoes, and contemporary stained glass.

⑧ Towers. The evolution of Gothic architecture was influenced by the cathedral's 12th-century towers, which can be climbed for sweeping views across the Beauce countryside. Architect Viollet-le-Duc considered the 105m (344-ft.) spire of the Old Bell Tower (also called the *Tour du Midi*) to be flawless. The Flamboyant Gothic New Bell Tower is one of the tallest in France. Huff and puff your way to the top and admire the village of Chartres's tiled rooftops. *Cloître Notre-Dame.* ☎ 02-37-31-22-07. http://cathedrale-chartres.monuments-nationaux.fr. Admission 7.50€. Mon–Sat 9:30am–12:30pm & 2pm–5pm (May–Sept until 6pm), Sun 2pm–5pm (May–Sept until 6pm). ●

Before You Go

Government Tourist Offices

In the U.S.: Atout France, 825 3rd Avenue, 29th floor, New York, NY 10022 (☎ 212/745-0952; info.us@ franceguide.com; http://us.france guide.com. **In Canada:** Atout France, 1800 Ave. McGill College, Ste. 1010, Montreal H3A 3J6 (☎ 514/288-2026; http://ca-en.franceguide.com). **In the U.K.:** Atout France, Lincoln House 300 High Holborn, London WC1V 7JH (☎ 09068/244-123; http://uk. franceguide.com). **In Ireland:** Office has now closed. Contact London on the details above or e-mail info.uk@ rendezvousenfrance.com. **In Australia:** French Tourist Bureau, 25 Bligh St., Sydney, NSW 2000 (☎ 02/9231-5244); info.au@franceguide.com; http://au.franceguide.com.

The Best Times to Go

Paris is less crowded in **August,** when the locals traditionally take their annual holiday. This is also a time for some of Paris's best outdoor festivals. However, cheaper hotels tend to fill up with students and budget travelers, and many (but by no means all) of the smaller shops, restaurants, and galleries close for 2 weeks at the beginning of the month. You may want to avoid **late September/early October,** when the annual auto show attracts thousands of enthusiasts. Spring in Paris is still a good time to come, but so too is December, when many hotels have special offers on the run up to Christmas—although you might not get any sunshine.

Weather

Generally speaking, summers are warm and pleasant, with only a few oppressively hot days. Although more and more hotels are adding air-conditioning to the rooms, many cheaper accommodations still get hot and stuffy. Rain is common throughout the year, especially in winter.

Useful Websites

- **www.parisinfo.com** and **www. nouveau-paris-ile-de-france.fr:** Comprehensive information about traveling to Paris and Île de France, including hotels, sightseeing, and notices of special events

- **www.mappy.fr** and **www. viamichelin.com:** Online maps and journey planner; covers Paris and the whole of France

- **www.pagesjaunes.fr:** Online phone directory for businesses and services

- **www.culture.fr:** Extensive listings of upcoming cultural events

- **www.parissi.com:** Guide to the Parisian music scene, with an emphasis on nightclubs

- **www.paris.fr:** The City Hall's guide to Paris, with museum and exhibition listings

Cell Phones (Mobile Phones)

If your phone has GSM (Global System for Mobiles) capability, and you have a world-compatible phone, you should be able to make and receive calls to and from France. Check with your service provider before you leave. Call and data charges can be high. Alternatively, you can rent a phone through **Roadpost** (www.roadpost.com), InTouch Global (www.intouchglobal.com), or **Cellhire** (www.cellhire.com; www.cellhire. co.uk; www.cellhire.com.au). After a simple online registration, one of these companies will ship a phone (usually with a U.K. number) to your home or office. Usage charges can be astronomical, so read the fine print.

U.K. mobiles work in France; call your service provider before departing your home country to ensure that the international call bar has been switched off and to check call charges, which can be extremely high. Also remember that you are charged for calls you *receive* on a U.K. mobile used abroad.

Car Rentals

There's very little need to rent a car in Paris, but if you're determined to do so, it's usually cheapest to book a car online before you leave your home country. Try **Hertz** (www.hertz. com), **Avis** (www.avis.com), or **Budget** (www.budget.com). If you're in the U.S., you should also consider **AutoEurope** (www.autoeurope.com), which sends you a prepaid voucher, thus locking in the exchange rate.

Getting **There**

By Plane

Paris has two international airports—**Orly** (☎ 39-50) and **Charles de Gaulle (CDG)** (☎ 39-50). At CDG, Air France flights arrive at Terminal 2, while most other flights come into Terminals 1 and 3. At Orly, international flights arrive at Orly Sud (South) and domestic flights at Orly Ouest (West). RER B operates between the two airports, with two stops for CDG: the first for T1 and T3, the second for T2. Orly's stop is Anthony; from there, a monorail takes you to the airport. (See "From Orly," below.)

From Charles de Gaulle: RER trains leave every 15 minutes (5am to approximately midnight) from the station near Terminal 3 (follow signs on foot from T3 or catch the free shuttles between terminals), serving several of the major downtown Métro stations including Gare du Nord (for Eurostar and Thalys) and Châtelet, the central hub (trip time: 35 min.). Air France also operates two shuttle-bus services into Paris: one departing every 12 minutes (5:35am–11pm) for Place d'Etoile and Porte Maillot, and the other every 30 minutes (7am–9:30pm) for Gare Montparnasse and Gare de Lyon (www.lescarsairfrance.com). A taxi to the city costs about 55€; the fare is higher at night (8pm–7am). The trip takes 40 to 50 minutes by bus or taxi.

From Orly: There are no direct trains to central Paris, but the airport is served by a **monorail** (Orlyval) that takes you to the RER station Anthony, where you can catch line B into the city (trip time about 30 min.). Air France buses leave from Orly Ouest and Orly Sud every 12 minutes (5:45am–11pm) for the Gare des Invalides, where you can catch a taxi or the Métro. A taxi from the airport into Paris costs about 45€ (more at night). It takes 25 minutes to an hour to get to Paris by bus or taxi, depending on traffic.

By Car

The main highways into Paris are the A-1 from the north (Great Britain and Benelux); A-13 from Rouen, Normandy, and northwest France; A-10 from Bordeaux, the Pyrenees, southwest France, and Spain; A-6 from Lyon, the French Alps, the Riviera, and Italy; and A-4 and A-5 from eastern France.

By Train

North Americans can buy a **Eurailpass** or individual tickets from most travel agencies, or at any office of **Rail Europe** (☎ 800/622-8600 in the U.S., 800/361-RAIL in Canada; www.raileurope.com). For details on the rail passes available in the U.K., call the **National Rail Inquiries,**

Victoria Station, London SW1V 1JZ (☎ 08457-484-950; www.nationalrail. co.uk). From the U.K., you can travel to Paris under the English Channel via the Eurostar (trip time about 2½ hr.). Buy tickets directly from **Eurostar** (☎ 08432-186-186 from the U.K., ☎ 44-1233-617-575 from outside the U.K., or ☎ 08-92-35-35-39 in France; www.eurostar.com).

By Bus

Bus travel to Paris is available from London and several other cities on the Continent. The arrival and departure point for Europe's largest bus operator, **Eurolines France** (www.eurolines.fr; ☎ 08-92-89-90-91 from France), is a 15- to 25-minute Métro ride from central Paris, at the terminus of Métro line 3 (Galleini). Because Eurolines doesn't have sales agents outside Europe, most non-European travelers wait until they reach England or the Continent to buy their tickets. Any European travel agent can arrange this for you, or you can book online at www.eurolines.co.uk (☎ 08/717-81-8181 from the U.K.). Before you travel between London and Paris by bus, check the Eurostar website for offers, as train tickets sometimes dip to as little as 66€ return—about 30€ more than a bus ticket, but you may find spending the extra cash worthwhile for the upgrade in comfort and speed.

Getting Around

Paris Orientation

Paris is encircled by the *périphérique*, a busy ring-road that loosely follows the city's former fortifications. It links the city center to its suburbs and France's highway system (*autoroutes*). Everything within the *périphérique* is classified as the city center. The River Seine runs east-west through it, splitting the city into the Right Bank (north of the Seine), and the Left Bank (south). Together, the Right and Left Banks are divided into 20 sectors called *arrondissements* with postcodes beginning with 75 (designating central Paris) and numbered from 1 to 20 (75001 to 75020; or abbreviated to 1st to 20th). The numbers spiral out clockwise, like the shell of a snail, starting at 1 (around the Louvre) and finishing at 20 (around Père Lachaise). In terms of atmosphere, arrondissements 1 to 8 cover most tourist sights, from the Louvre and Notre-Dame, to the Eiffel Tower and the Champs-Elysées. Literary Paris, with its cafes and the Sorbonne University, is concentrated around the 5th and 6th. The 9th to 11th and 17th to 20th are the city's trendiest areas (including the Canal St-Martin, Montmartre, and the Père Lachaise cemetery), although some parts may look shabby. Avoid La Chapelle and Barbès-Rochechouart (18th) at night. The 12th to 16th are largely residential areas but still have plenty of bars and restaurants. The 13th is where you'll find the city's main Chinese quarter. The 16th is very chic, with grand buildings and prices to match.

Getting Around by Public Transportation

The **Métro** network is vast, reliable, and cheap, and within Paris you can transfer between the subway and the **RER** (Réseau Express Régional) regional trains at no extra cost. The Métro runs from 5:30am to 12:30am Sunday to Thursday (until 1:30am Fri–Sat and the night before public holidays; 2am on line 2). Detailed information is at www.ratp.fr.

The Métro is reasonably safe at any hour, but use your common sense and be on your guard for pickpockets. Châtelet-les-Halles RER is best avoided at night, as troublemakers tend to loiter there. For ticket advice, see below.

Buses are slower than the Métro but reliable and offer sightseeing opportunities. Most buses run from 7am to 8:30pm, after which a nighttime service covers key areas until 5:30am. Services are limited on Sunday and public holidays. At certain stops, signs list the destinations and numbers of the buses serving that point. Bus and Métro fares are the same (although each requires a separate ticket), and you can use the same tickets on both.

Trams are the latest addition to the network. There are three lines in central Paris (T2, T3a, and T3b), which run around the outskirts of the city, roughly following the *périphérique* (ring-road). Tram fare is the same as on the Métro and on buses, but you will need a separate ticket.

Buying Tickets

Single journey tickets, or packs of 10 tickets (un carnet, pronounced car-*nay*) can be bought from a machine in the subway station (with cash or a credit card). Individual tickets cost 1.70€ (2€, if you buy directly from a bus driver) and a pack of 10 is 13.30€ (prices as of press time; they may be higher once you get there). If you plan to ride the Métro a lot, the Paris Visite pass (☎ 32-46; www. ratp.info/touristes; available from all RATP desks in the Métro and from tourist offices) may be worthwhile. You get unlimited rides for 1, 2, 3, or 5 days for access to zones 1 to 3, which includes central Paris and its nearby suburbs, or zones 1 to 6, which includes Disneyland (zone 5), Versailles (zone 4), and the Charles de Gaulle (zone 5) and Orly (zone 4) airports. It is valid only from the first

time you use it, so you can buy it in advance. Remember to fill in your name (and your children's names) as well as the series number on the card and the date of its first use. Prices range from 10.55€ to 57.75€, depending on the zone covered and the number of days.

Another discount pass is Carte Mobilis, which allows unlimited travel on bus, subway, and RER lines during a 1-day period for 6.50€ to 15.65€, depending on the zone. Ask for it at any Métro station. You will also need a passport photo for each family member.

By Taxi

You can hail a taxi when its sign reads LIBRE or if it sports a full green or white light. The flag drops at 5.10€, and from 7am to 7pm you pay 1€ per kilometer (or 1.20€ the rest of the time). Cabs are scarce during rush hour and when the Métro closes. Unlicensed cabs (which are usually just a person with a car) may seem like a cheap alternative (especially at the airport), but don't use them under any circumstances. You could find yourself the victim of a robbery— or worse. If you'd like to hire a taxi with a chauffeur for a single journey or even the whole day, try **Paris Moving,** a friendly, reliable service run by husband-and-wife duo Fabrice and Gwladys Grüngrass (22 bd. des Filles du Calvaire, 75011; ☎ 06-60-45-21-50 or 06-24-27-10-50; gwladys@paris moving.com). Other options are **Les Taxis Bleus** (☎ 36-09; www.taxis-bleus.com) or **Taxi G7** (☎ 36-07; www.taxisg7.fr); call ☎ 36-49 if you want an eco-friendly taxi.

By Car

Driving in Paris is not recommended. Parking is difficult, traffic is dense, and networks of one-way streets make navigation, even with the best of maps, a problem. You would be much better off making use of the extensive public transport system or taking cabs.

By Foot

The best way to take in the city is to walk. The center is very pedestrian-friendly, and so long as you follow all the usual rules of thumb—buy a good map or phone app (or carry this guide with you) and stick to busy, well-lit places at night—you're bound to make a few unexpected discoveries along the way.

By Bike

Paris does have cycle paths, even if you have to compete with heavy traffic, and it's a fine way to sightsee.

The best deal for short journeys is the **Vélib,** Paris's excellent self-service bike scheme, available 24/7. A subscription is 1.70€ for 1 day and 8€ for 1 week. You can take a

bike from any stand (there are more than 20,000 across the city), use it, replace it, and take a new one (you can even buy a ticket online at http://en.velib.paris.fr). If a rack is full, check the map on the service point for the nearest stand. Tickets can be bought with your credit card at any service point. You'll have to authorize a 150€ deposit, which will be taken from your card only if the bike is not returned, and type in a PIN of your choice. The machine will give you a card with a code that you can use to unlock the bikes.

The first 30 minutes are free. Every additional 30 minutes costs 1€ extra (i.e., if you keep the bike for 6 hours, you'll pay an extra 12€; but if you return it to a stand every 30 min. and wait 5 min. before taking out a new one, you'll pay only the subscription fee).

Fast Facts

APARTMENT RENTALS In Paris, **Alcôve & Agapes** (☎ 01-44-85-06-05; www.bed-and-breakfast-in-paris.com) promotes upmarket B&B accommodations. **Good Morning Paris** (☎ 01-47-07-28-29; www.goodmorningparis.fr) also has more than 100 rooms in the city, plus apartments for two to four people (99€–125€); or try the excellent **Hôtes Qualité Paris** (www.hotesqualiteparis.fr), with apartments approved by the City of Paris for rental.

The U.K.-based **Alastair Sawdays** (www.sawdays.co.uk) also offers an excellent collection of charming B&Bs and tourist apartments in Paris. **New York Habitat** (☎ 212/255-8018; paris@nyhabitat.com; www.nyhabitat.com) rents furnished apartments and vacation accommodations in Paris and the south of France. **Airbnb** (www.airbnb.com)—an Internet community—is also a

good source for private vacation rentals, offering direct contact with residents across Paris.

ATMS/CASHPOINTS The easiest and best way to get cash abroad is through an ATM—the **Cirrus** and **PLUS** networks span the globe. Most banks charge a fee for international withdrawals—check with your bank before you leave home.

BABYSITTERS Most expensive and some moderately priced hotels offer babysitting services, usually subcontracted to local agencies and requiring at least 24 hours' notice. You usually pay the sitter directly, and rates average 10€ to 13€ per hour. One good agency is **Baby Sitting Services** (1 place Paul Verlaine, 92100 Boulogne, Billancourt; ☎ 01-46-21-33-16; www.babysittingservices.fr). Specify when calling that you need a sitter who speaks English. Also try the American Church's basement bulletin board, where English-speaking (often American) students post notices to offer babysitting services. The church is at 65 quai d'Orsay, 7th (☎ 01-45-62-05-00; www.acparis.org; Métro: Invalides).

BANKS Most banks are open Monday to Friday from 9am to 5pm and on Saturday mornings. Most hotels will cash traveler's checks, but most banks and foreign exchanges will give you a better rate.

BUSINESS HOURS Shops tend to be open from 9:30am to 7pm, but opening hours can be a little erratic. Some traditional shops open at 8am and close at 8 or 9pm, but the lunch break can last up to 3 hours, starting at 1pm. Most museums close 1 day a week (Mon or Tues) and on some national holidays.

CONSULATES & EMBASSIES **U.S. Embassy,** 2 av. Gabriel, 8th (☎ 01-43-12-22-22, http://france.usembassy.gov); **Canadian Embassy,** 35 av. Montaigne, 8th (☎ 01-44-43-29-00, www.canadainternational.gc.ca); **U.K. Embassy,** 35 rue Faubourg St-Honoré, 8th (☎ 01-44-51-31-00, www.gov.uk/government/world/france); **U.K. Consulate,** 16 bis rue d'Anjou, 8th (☎ 01-44-51-31-02); **Irish Embassy,** 12 av. Foch, 16th (☎ 01-44-17-67-00, www.embassyofireland.fr); **Australian Embassy,** 4 rue Jean-Ray, 15th (☎ 01-40-59-33-00, www.france.embassy.gov.au); **New Zealand Embassy,** 7ter rue Lêonard-de-Vinci, 16th (☎ 01-45-01-43-43, www.nzembassy.com).

CREDIT CARDS Credit cards are a safe way to carry money. They also provide a convenient record of all your expenses, and they generally offer good exchange rates. You can also withdraw cash advances from your credit cards at banks or ATMs (cashpoints), provided you know your PIN. Keep in mind that when you use your credit card abroad, most banks charge a fee.

CURRENCY EXCHANGE Cash your traveler's checks at banks or foreign exchange offices. Some hotels and post offices (La Poste) change traveler's checks or convert money as well. Currency exchanges are also found at Paris airports and train stations and along most of the major boulevards. The currency exchange cashiers along Avenue de l'Opéra often offer the best rates.

CUSTOMS Customs restrictions for visitors entering France differ for citizens of the European Union and for citizens of non-E.U. countries.

For U.S. Citizens For specifics on what you can bring back from your trip to France, download the invaluable free pamphlet Know Before You Go online at www.cbp.gov, or contact U.S. Customs Border Protection (CBP), (☎ 877/CBP-5511, or 202/983-8000 from abroad).

For Canadian Citizens For a clear summary of Canadian rules, call for the booklet I Declare, issued by the Canada Customs and Revenue Agency (☎ 800/461-9999 in Canada, or 204/983-3500 from outside Canada; www.cbsa-asfc.gc.ca).

For U.K. Citizens For more information, contact **HM Revenue & Customs** at ☎ 0300/200-3700, or consult the website www.hmrc.gov.uk or www.gov.uk/browse/business/imports-exports.

For Australian Citizens A helpful brochure available from Australian consulates or customs offices is Know Before You Go. For more information, call the **Australian Customs Service** at ☎ 1300/363-263, (61/2 9313-3010 from outside Australia) or go to www.customs.gov.au.

For New Zealand Citizens Request the free pamphlet New Zealand Customs Guide for Travelers, Notice no. 4, from New Zealand Customs Service, The Customhouse, 17–21 Whitmore St., Box 2218, Wellington (☎ 0800/428-786;

The Savvy Traveler

or 64/9 927-8036 from overseas; www.customs.govt.nz).

DENTISTS See "Emergencies," below.

DOCTORS See "Emergencies," below.

DRUGSTORES After regular hours, ask at your hotel where the nearest 24-hour pharmacy is. You'll also find the address posted on the doors or windows of other drugstores in the neighborhood. One all-night drugstore is **Pharmacie Les Champs,** 84 av. des Champs-Elysées, 8th (☎ 01-45-62-02-41, www.pharmacieleschamps.fr).

ELECTRICITY France uses the 220-volt system (two round prongs), so you will need an adapter for all electronic equipment (cell phone, computer, etc.). If you can't find one in your home country, you should be able to pick one up at the airport or in almost any Paris supermarket.

EMERGENCIES For the **police**, call ☎ 17. To report a **fire**, call ☎ 18. For an **ambulance**, call the fire department at ☎ 18, or the S.A.M.U. ambulance company at ☎ 15. From anywhere in Europe, including France, the **general emergency number** is ☎ 112. If you need non-urgent medical attention, practitioners in most fields can be found at the Centre Médical Europe, 44 rue d'Amsterdam, 9th (☎ 01-42-81-93-33; www.centre-medical-europe.com). For **emergency dental service**, call S.O.S. Dentaire, ☎ 01-43-36-36-00. **Hospitals with English-speaking staff** are Hôpital Américain, 63 bd. Victor Hugo, Neuilly-sur-Seine (92) (☎ 01-46- 41-25-25; www.american-hospital.org), and Hôpital Franco Britannique, 3 rue Barbes, Levallois Perret (92) (☎ 01-47-59-59-59; www.ihfb.org).

U.K. nationals will need a European Health Insurance Card (EHIC) to receive free or reduced-cost health benefits during a visit to a European Economic Area (EEA) country (European Union countries plus Iceland, Liechtenstein, and Norway) or Switzerland.

The quickest way to apply for one in the U.K. is online (www.ehic.org.uk), call ☎ 0300/3301-350 (44-191-218-1999 from abroad), or get a form from the post office. You still pay upfront for treatment and related expenses; the doctor will give you a form to reclaim most of the money (about 70% of doctor's fees and 35–65% of medicines/prescription charges), which you should send off while still in France (see the EHIC website for details, or see www.dh.gov.uk/travellers). Non-E.U. nationals—with the exception of Canadians, who have the same rights as E.U. citizens to medical treatment in France—need comprehensive travel insurance that covers medical treatment overseas. Even then, you pay bills upfront and apply for a refund.

EVENT LISTINGS *L'Officiel des Spectacle* (sold in newspaper kiosks and consultable online; www.offi.fr) provides listings of everything that's going on in the city. Another handy website is http://spectacles.premiere.fr. *Le Figaro* carries a special listings supplement every Wednesday. Or try the online magazines **Gogo Paris** (www.gogoparis.com) and *Time Out Paris* (www.timeout.com/paris/en).

FAMILY TRAVEL The official website of the French Tourist Board, Atout France (http://int.rendez-vousenfrance.com/en) has sections on family travel. The website www.france4families.com is a very useful resource, with lots of general information about France from a family perspective, plus guides to all regions, including Paris. If your trip to Paris is part of a wider tour of France, another good site is http://totstotravel.co.uk, which details family-friendly properties to rent outside Paris and gives valuable info about traveling in France with children, including tips on what to pack and baggage allowances on airlines.

GAY & LESBIAN TRAVELERS A hot line (SOS Homophobie) offering counseling for persons with gay-related problems is ☎ 08-10-10-81-35 or 01-48-06-42-41 (www.sos-homo phobie.org). **La Maison des Femmes** (☎ 01-43-43-41-13; http://maisondesfemmes.free.fr) offers information about Paris for lesbians. Paris's largest gay bookstore is **Les Mots à la Bouche,** 6 rue Ste-Croix-de-la-Bretonnerie, 4th (☎ 01-42-78-88-30; www.motsbouche.com).

HOLIDAYS Public holidays include New Year's Day (Jan 1), Easter Monday (Mar or Apr), Labor Day (May 1), Victory Day 1945 (May 8), Ascension Day (40 days after Easter), Whit Monday (11 days after Ascension Day), National Day/Bastille Day (July 14), Assumption Day (Aug 15), All Saints' Day (Nov 1), Armistice Day 1918 (Nov 11), and Christmas Day (Dec 25).

INSURANCE North Americans with homeowner's or renter's insurance are probably covered for lost luggage. If not, inquire with **Travel Assistance International** (☎ 800/643-5525; http://travelassistance international.com) or **Travelex** (☎ 800/228-9792; www.travelex insurance.com). These insurers can also provide trip-cancellation, medical, and emergency evacuation coverage abroad. The website www.moneysupermarket.com compares prices across a wide range of providers for single- and multitrip policies. **For U.K. citizens,** insurance is always advisable, even if you have an EHIC form. (See "Emergencies," above.)

INTERNET ACCESS Most hotels offer Internet access (usually at a price) and many are equipped with both Wi-Fi and a computer; alternatively, many cafes offer Wi-Fi. There are also more than 260 free Wi-Fi spots dotted around the city (check www.paris.fr for details). To surf the Net or check your e-mail, try **Milk;** one of several locations is 28 rue du 4 septembre, 2nd (☎ 01-40-06-00-70; www.milklub.com).

LIQUOR LAWS Supermarkets, grocery stores, and cafes sell alcoholic beverages. The legal drinking age is 18. Hours of cafes vary; some even stay open 24 hours. It's illegal to drive while drunk. If convicted, motorists face a stiff fine and a possible prison term.

LOST PROPERTY If your luggage is lost, immediately file a lost-luggage claim at the airport, detailing the luggage contents. For most airlines, you must report delayed, damaged, or lost baggage within 4 hours of arrival. If you lose any belongings in Paris, try the **Service des Objets Trouvés** (Lost-Property Bureau), 36 rue des Morillons, 15th (☎ 08-21-00-25-25), which collects everything that is found in the city. You might be lucky.

MAIL/POST OFFICES Most post offices (La Poste) in Paris are open Monday through Friday from 8am to 7pm and Saturday from 8am to noon. However, the **main post office,** at 52 rue du Louvre (☎ 36-31, www.laposte.fr), is open 24 hours a day for stamps, phone calls, and sending faxes and telegrams. Stamps can usually be purchased from your hotel reception desk and at cafes with red TABAC signs.

MONEY The currency of France is the euro, which can be used in most other E.U. countries. The exchange rate varies, but at press time, 1 euro was equal to US$1.30 and £0.85. The best way to get cash in Paris is at ATMs or cashpoints (see above). Credit cards are accepted at almost all shops, restaurants, and hotels (although not always American Express or Diner's Club), but you should always have some cash on hand for incidentals and sightseeing admissions. Most taxis accept credit cards. Check with the driver, or request a card-payment taxi when you reserve.

NEWSPAPERS & MAGAZINES English-language newspapers are available from most kiosks, including the American *International Herald Tribune* and *USA Today* and the British *Times*, *Guardian*, and *Independent*. The leading French-language domestic papers are *Le Monde*, *Le Figaro*, and *Libération*.

PASSPORTS If your passport is lost or stolen, contact your country's embassy or consulate immediately. (See "Consulates & Embassies," above.) Before you travel, you should copy the critical pages and keep them in a separate place.

POLICE Call ☎ **17** for emergencies. The principal *Préfecture* (police station) is at 9 bd. du Palais, 4th (☎ 01-53-71-53-71; www.prefecturedepolice.interieur.gouv.fr; Métro: Cité).

SAFETY The center of Paris is relatively safe. Look out for pickpockets—especially child pickpockets. Their method is to get very close to a target, ask for a handout, and deftly help themselves to your money or passport. Robbery at gun- or knife-point is rare, but not unknown. For more information, consult the U.S. State Department's website at www.travel.state.gov; in the U.K., consult the Foreign Office's website, www.fco.gov.uk; and in Australia, consult the government travel advisory service at www.smartraveller.gov.au.

SENIOR TRAVELERS Mention that you're a senior when you make your travel reservations. As in most cities, people over the age of 60 qualify for reduced admission to theaters, museums, and other attractions as well as discounted fares on public transportation.

SMOKING Smoking is now illegal in public places (including restaurants, bars, theaters, and public transportation) but is tolerated outside and on cafe terraces. Some hotels still provide smokers' bedrooms (so ask when making reservations); otherwise, they may fine you for smoking in a nonsmoking room.

TAXES Value Added Tax, or VAT (TVA in French) is 19.6 percent, but non-E.U. visitors can get a refund when they spend 175.01€ or more in any store that participates in the VAT refund program. The shops will give you a form, which you must get stamped at Customs. (Allow extra time.) Mark the paperwork to request a credit card refund; otherwise you'll be stuck with a check in euros. An option is to ask for a **Global Refund form** (☎ 00800/32-111-111, 00800/32-222-555, or 421-232-111-111 outside France; www.globalblue.com) when you make your purchase and take it to a Global Refund counter at the airport. Your money is refunded on the spot, minus a commission.

TELEPHONES Public phones are found in cafes, some Métro stations, post offices, and on the street. Coin-operated telephones are rare. Most phones take *télécartes*, prepaid calling cards available at kiosks and post offices. Their cost ranges from about 8€ to 16€, depending on how many units you buy. To make a **direct international call,** first dial 00, then dial the country code, the area code (minus the first zero), and the local number. The country code for the **U.S. and Canada** is 1; **Great Britain,** 44; **Ireland,** 353; **Australia,** 61; and **New Zealand,** 64. You can also call the U.S., Canada, the U.K., Ireland, Australia, or New Zealand using **AT&T World Connect,** which allows you to avoid hotel surcharges; from within France, dial ☎ **0800/99-00-11-10-11** and then follow the prompts.

TICKETS There are many theater ticket agencies in Paris, but buying tickets directly from the box office or at a discount agency can be up to 50 percent cheaper. Try **Kiosque Théâtre,** 15 place de la Madeleine, 8th; in front of Gare de Montparnasse, 14th; or Place des Ternes, 17th (www.kiosquetheatre.com). Tickets for many shows, sports events, and tours can also be purchased in advance in your home country through your travel agent; try **Keith Prowse** (www.keithprowse.com) for advance tickets to cabaret events and guided visits but expect to pay a commission fee.

TIPPING In cafes and restaurants, waiter service is included, although you can round the bill up or leave some small change, if you like. The same goes for taxi drivers. In more expensive hotels, a tip of 1€ to 2€ for having luggage carried by a hotel porter is appreciated but not an obligation.

TOILETS If you use a toilet at a cafe or brasserie, it's customary to make some small purchase. In the street, the domed self-cleaning lavatories are an option if you have small change. Some Métro stations have public toilets, but the degree of cleanliness varies. Be prepared—in some places, the facilities on offer may be nothing more than a porcelain hole in the floor.

TOURIST OFFICES For tourist information, try **Office du Tourisme,** 25 rue des Pyramides, 1st (www.parisinfo.com.).

TOURS The two largest tour companies are **Globus/Cosmos** (www.globusandcosmos.com) and **Trafalgar** (☎ 866/513-1995; www.trafalgartours.com). Many major airlines offer air/land package deals that include tours of Paris; ask the airlines or your travel agent for details.

TRAVELERS WITH DISABILITIES Nearly all modern hotels in France now have rooms designed for people with disabilities, but many older hotels do not, so check when booking. Most high-speed trains within France have wheelchair access, and guide dogs ride free. Paris's Métro and RER system does have some elevator access, but it is very difficult to use if you're in a wheelchair. **Paris Info** (www.parisinfo.com) has resources for travelers with disabilities, including a list of accessible hotels. The **Association des Paralysés de France** (☎ 01-40-78-69-00; www.apf.asso.fr) provides help for individuals who use wheelchairs. Organizations that offer a vast range of resources and assistance to travelers with disabilities include **MossRehab** (☎ 800/CALL-MOSS [225-5667]; www.mossresourcenet.org); the **American Foundation for the Blind** (AFB; ☎ 800/232-5463; www.afb.org); and **Society for Accessible Travel & Hospitality** (SATH; ☎ 212/447-7284; www.sath.org). **AirAmbulanceCard.com**(☎ 877/424-7633) is now partnered with SATH and allows you to preselect top-notch hospitals in case of an emergency.

Access-Able Travel Source (www.access-able.com) offers a comprehensive database on travel agents around the world with experience in accessible travel; destination-specific access information; and links to such resources as service animals, equipment rentals, and access guides.

Flying with Disability (www.flying-with-disability.org) is a comprehensive information source on airplane travel. The "Accessible Travel" link at www.mobility-advisor.com offers a variety of travel resources to persons with disabilities. Also check out the quarterly magazine **Emerging Horizons** (www.emerginghorizons.com), available by subscription.

British travelers should contact **Tourism for All** (☎ 0845-124-9971 in the U.K. only; www.tourismforall.org.uk) to access a wide range of travel information and resources for elderly people and those with disabilities.

For more on organizations that offer resources to travelers with disabilities, go to Frommers.com.

Paris: **A Brief History**

2000 B.C. The Parisii tribe founds the settlement of Lutétia alongside the Seine.

52 B.C. Julius Caesar conquers Lutétia during the Gallic wars.

300 A.D. Lutétia is renamed Paris. Roman power begins to weaken in France.

1422 England invades Paris during the Hundred Years' War.

1429 Joan of Arc tries to regain Paris for the French; she is later burned at the stake by the English in Rouen.

1572 The wars of religion reach their climax with the St. Bartholomew's Day massacre of Protestants.

1598 Henri IV endorses the Edict of Nantes, granting tolerance to Protestants.

1643 Louis XIV moves his court to the newly built Versailles.

1789 The French Revolution begins.

1793 Louis XVI and his queen, Marie Antoinette, are publicly guillotined.

1799 A coup d'état installs Napoleon Bonaparte as head of government.

1804 Napoleon declares France an empire and is crowned emperor at Notre-Dame.

1804–15 The Napoleonic wars are fought.

1814 Paris is briefly occupied by a coalition, including Britain and Russia. The Bourbon monarchy is restored.

1848 Revolutions occur across Europe. King Louis-Philippe is deposed by the autocratic Napoleon III.

1860S The Impressionist style of painting emerges.

1870–71 The Franco-Prussian War ends in the siege of Paris. The Third Republic is established, while much of the city is controlled by the revolutionary Paris Commune.

1914–18 World War I rips apart Europe. Millions are killed in the trenches of northeast France.

1940 German troops occupy France during World War II. The French Resistance under General Charles de Gaulle maintains symbolic headquarters in London.

1944 U.S. troops liberate Paris; de Gaulle returns in triumph.

1958 France's Fourth Republic collapses. General de Gaulle is called out of retirement to head the Fifth Republic.

1968 Parisian students and factory workers engage in a general revolt; the government is overhauled in the aftermath.

1994 François Mitterrand and Queen Elizabeth II open the Channel Tunnel.

1995 Jacques Chirac is elected president over François Mitterrand. Paris is crippled by a general strike.

2002 The euro replaces the franc as France's national currency.

2003–04 French opposition to the war in Iraq causes the largest diplomatic rift with America in decades.

2007 Nicolas Sarkozy replaces Jacques Chirac as president of France.

2012 Socialist François Hollande is elected president over Sarkozy.

2013 Gay marriage is legalized.French

Architecture

This section serves as a guide to some of the architectural styles you'll see in Paris. However, it's worth pointing out that very few buildings (especially churches) were built in one particular style. These massive, expensive structures often took centuries to complete, during which time tastes changed and plans were altered.

Romanesque (800–1100)

Taking their inspiration from ancient Rome, the Romanesque architects concentrated on building large churches with wide aisles. Few examples of the Romanesque style remain in Paris, but the church of **Saint-Germain-des-Prés** (oldest part, 6th century A.D.) is a good example. The overall building is Romanesque, but by the time builders got to creating the choir, the early Gothic was on— note the pointy arches.

Gothic (1100–1500)

By the 12th century, engineering developments freed church architecture from the thick, heavy walls of Romanesque structures.

Instead of dark, somber, relatively unadorned Romanesque interiors that forced the eyes of the faithful toward the altar, the Gothic interior enticed the churchgoers' gaze upward to high ceilings filled with light. The squat, brooding Romanesque exteriors were replaced by graceful buttresses and spires. Arguably the finest example of Gothic church architecture anywhere in the world is **Notre-Dame** (1163–1250).

Renaissance (1500–1630)

In architecture, as in painting, the Renaissance came from Italy and took some time to coalesce. And, as in painting, its rules stressed proportion, order, classical inspiration, and precision, resulting in unified, balanced structures. The 1544 **Hôtel Carnavalet** (23 rue de Sévigné), a Renaissance mansion,

exemplifies the style. It now contains the **Musée Carnavalet** (p 62), a museum devoted to the history of Paris and the French Revolution.

Baroque, Rococo, and Neoclassical (1630–1800)

During the reign of Louis XIV (1643–1715), art and architecture were subservient to political ends. French Baroque buildings were grandiose and severely ordered— Versailles is the best model. Opulence was especially pronounced in interior decoration, which increasingly became the excessively detailed and self-indulgent rococo (*rocaille* in French) style. Rococo tastes didn't last long, though, and soon a neoclassical movement was raising such structures as Paris's **Panthéon** (1758), based even more strictly on ancient models than the earlier Renaissance classicism was.

The 19th Century

Architectural styles in 19th-century Paris were eclectic, beginning in a severe classical mode and ending with something of an identity crisis—torn between Industrial Age technology and Art Nouveau's organic vibe. During the reign of Emperor Napoleon III (1852–1870), classicism was reinterpreted in an ornate, dramatic mode. Urban planning was the architectural rage, and Paris became a city of wide boulevards courtesy of **Baron Georges-Eugène Haussmann** (1809–91), commissioned by Napoleon III in 1852 to modernize the city. Paris owes much of its remarkably unified look to Haussmann.

Expositions in 1878, 1889, and 1900 were the catalysts for constructing huge glass-and-steel structures that showed off modern techniques. This produced such Parisian monuments as the **Eiffel Tower** and **Gare d'Orsay** (which now houses the Musée d'Orsay). However, the subsequent emergence of the Art Nouveau movement was, in many ways, a rebellion against the late-19th-century industrial zeal. Peaking around the turn of the century, it celebrated curvaceous asymmetrical designs, often based on plants and flowers. It was during this short period that the famous Art Nouveau **Métro station entrances** were designed by **Hector Guimard** (1867–1942); the **Porte Dauphine** (line 2) and **Abbesses** (line 12) entrances are the most intact examples today. But the city's finest Art Nouveau structure is the intricately decorated apartment block at 29 av. de Rapp in the 7th.

The 20th Century

The ravages of war stalled the progress of French architecture for a number of decades, but the latter half of the 20th century saw some of the most audacious architectural projects in French history—and certainly some of the most controversial. It has taken decades for such structures as the **Centre Pompidou** or the **Louvre**'s glass pyramids to become accepted by most Parisians, but now they are a well-loved part of the skyline.

The 21st Century

The face of Paris is ever-changing. The new era has already seen the arrival of the **Musée du Quai Branly** (2006), an impressive angular structure designed by Jean Nouvel, whose bright colors and clever use of vegetation are a flagship for 21st-century architecture within the city center. The sleek **Passerelle Simone de Beauvoir** bridge (2006) is another new addition, linking the Bercy district to the François Mitterrand library's towers. West of Paris in the **La Defense business district,** the fight is on to give the metropolitan area a cluster of skyscrapers, and back in the center, architect David Mangin has begun work on the brand-new **Les Halles** district (including a park and underground shopping mall), which should be complete in 2016. The most recent addition to the Louvre museum is a stark, modern structure—nicknamed the *libéllule* (dragonfly), after its undulating roof—in the Cours Visconti. Designed by Mario Bellini and Rudi Ricciotti, it houses the museum's Islamic art collections.

Useful Phrases & Menu Terms

It's amazing how often a word or two of halting French will change your host's disposition. At the very least, try to learn basic greetings, and—above all—the life-raft phrase, *Parlez-vous anglais?* ("Do you speak English?")

Useful Words and Phrases

ENGLISH	FRENCH	PRONUNCIATION
Yes/No	Oui/Non	wee/noh
Okay	D'accord	dah-core

ENGLISH	FRENCH	PRONUNCIATION
Please	S'il vous plaît	seel voo play
Thank you	Merci	mair-see
You're welcome	De rien	duh ree-ehn
Hello (during daylight)	Bonjour	bohn-jhoor
Good evening	Bonsoir	bohn-swahr
Good-bye	Au revoir	o ruh-vwahr
What's your name?	Comment vous appellez-vous?	kuh-mahn voo za-pell-ay-voo?
My name is	Je m'appelle	jhuh ma-pell
How are you?	Comment allez-vous?	kuh-mahn tahl-ay-voo?
So-so	Comme ci, comme ça	kum-see, kum-sah
I'm sorry/Excuse me	Pardon	pahr-dohn
Do you speak English?	Parlez-vous anglais?	par-lay-voo zahn-glay?
I don't speak French	Je ne parle pas français	jhuh ne parl pah frahn-say
I don't understand	Je ne comprends pas	jhuh ne kohm-prahn pas
Where is . . . ?	Où est . . . ?	ooh eh . . . ?
Why?	Pourquoi?	poor-kwah?
Here/There	ici/là	ee-see/lah
Left/Right	à gauche/à droite	a goash/a drwaht
Straight ahead	tout droit	too drwah

Food, Menu & Cooking Terms

ENGLISH	FRENCH	PRONUNCIATION
I would like	Je voudrais	jhe voo-dray
to eat	manger	mahn-jhay
Please give me	Donnez-moi, s'il vous plaît	doe-nay-mwah, seel voo play
a bottle of	une bouteille de	ewn boo-tay duh
a cup of	une tasse de	ewn tass duh
a glass of	un verre de	uh vair duh
a cocktail	un apéritif	uh ah-pay-ree-teef
the check/bill	l'addition/la note	la-dee-see-ohn/la noat
a knife	un couteau	uh koo-toe
a napkin	une serviette	ewn sair-vee-et
a spoon	une cuillère	ewn kwee-air
a fork	une fourchette	ewn four-shet
a fixed-price menu	un menu	uh may-new
Is the tip/service included?	Est-ce que le service est compris?	ess-ke luh ser-vees eh com-pree?
Waiter!/Waitress!	Monsieur!/Mademoiselle!	mun-syuh/mad-mwa-zel
Wine list	une carte des vins	ewn cart day van
Appetizer	une entrée	ewn en-tray
Main course	un plat principal	uh plah pran-see-pahl
Tip included	service compris	sehr-vees cohm-pree
Tasting/Chef's menu	menu dégustation	may-new day-gus-ta-see-on

Index

Photo Credits